# Stopwatch

Student's Book & Workbook

4

Simon Brewster

Richmond

**Richmond**
58 St Aldates
Oxford
OX1 1ST
United Kingdom

Publisher: *Justine Piekarowicz*
Editorial Team: *Suzanne Guerrero*
Art and Design Coordinators: *Karla Avila*
Design: *Karla Avila*
Layout: *Jaime Angeles, Karla Avila*
Pre-Press Coordinator: *Daniel Santillán*
Pre-Press Team: *Susana Alcántara, Virginia Arroyo*
Cover Design: *Karla Avila*
Cover Photograph: © **Thinkstock.com** *mezzotint* (female sprinters start)

**Illustrations:** Ismael Vásquez p. 16, 24, 31, 56, 57, 59, 87, 94, 99, 110, 122; Tomas Benitez p. 28, 29, 44, 45; Fabian de Jesus Ramírez p. 72, 78; Berenice Muñiz p. 59

**Photos:** © **Shutterstock.com:** a katz p. 13 (bottom center), Karves p. 13 (top center), Mitch Gunn p. 13 (Inter players with the trophy), windmoon p. 13 (Lion Dance), a katz p. 14 (top right), Png Studio Photography p. 14 (School Marching Band), lev radin p. 16 (top right), Markus Gebauer p. 23 (bottom right), Valeriya Anufriyeva p. 34 (top center), Dietmar Temps p. 34 (Unidentified traditional healer), Jordi C p. 35 (members of a nigerian family), J. Henning Buchholz p. 48 (Sumo wrestler), Kasia Soszka p. 48 (Maneki-neko cat figurine), Tinxi p. 55 (take part in the Star Wars Parade), Aspen Photo p. 55 (cheer), Leonard Zhukovsky p. 55 (Novak Djokovic), robert cicchetti p. 55 (customers outside the Apple Store), cjmacer p. 56 (Lego minifigure businessman), Bubbers BB p. 56 (Lego minifigure Batman), hitch3r p. 56 (Wolf Hoffmann and Peter Baltes), Settawat Udom p. 58 (bottom left), Lauren Elisabeth p. 59 (top right), StonePhotos p. 61 (Union Pacific Freight Train), imranahmedsg p. 62 (Men playing cricket), JStone p. 62 (Malala), JASON TENCH p. 64 (championship banners), David Persson p. 64 (celebrates the Stanley cup victory), littleny p. 64 (Fans await entry), Matt Trommer p. 64 (pitcher), Kevin M. Kerfoot p. 65 (Museo De

Impressão e Acabamento:EGB-Editora Gráfica Bernardi
Lote:259870

**Dados Internacionais de Catalogação na Publicação (CIP)**
**(Câmara Brasileira do Livro, SP, Brasil)**

Brewster, Simon
Stopwatch 4 : student's book & workbook / Simon Brewster. — São Paulo : Moderna, 2018.

1. Inglês - Estudo e ensino I. Título.

17-09955 CDD-420.7

**Índices para catálogo sistemático:**
1. Inglês : Estudo e ensino 420.7

**ISBN 978-85-16-10906-6**



**Richmond**
Editora Moderna Ltda.
Rua Padre Adelino, 758 - Belenzinho
São Paulo - SP - Brasil - CEP 03303-904
Central de atendimento ao usuário: 0800 771 8181
www.richmond.com.br
2018

Printed in Brazil

la Ciencia De Boston), Steve Lovegrove p. 67 (top left), Tinxi p. 68 (top right), Vania Georgieva p. 69 (roller coaster), Kenneth Sponsler p. 73 (Main Street), evantravels p. 76 (unidentified aborigines actor), Stanislav Fosenbauer p. 76 (ULURU KATA TJUTA NATIONAL PARK), Everett Collection p. 79 (Barack Obama), Denys Prykhodov p. 79 (iPad mini), Steven Collins p. 79 (ola gigante arrastra autos), Lucian Milasan p. 79 (London Olympics logo), Zeynep Demir p. 79 (iPhone 6), Oleg Golovnev p. 79 (Harry Potter), Tupungato p. 84 (La Rotonde restaurant), UKRID p. 84 (Cartoon Network Amazone), Ivan Garcia p. 84 (Ocuslus Rift), Paolo Bona p. 89 (AC Milan players), Aquarimage p. 89 (sailors sailing), Nikirov p. 89 (simulator skydiving glasses), peuceta p. 93 (musical group medieval), BlackMac p. 93 (Medieval parade), Vladimir Wrangel p. 93 (Medieval jousting), Sorbis p. 94 (Travelex counter) (train on RER station of Aeroport), Sean Locke Photography p. 95 (Opening Bottle), Maria_Janus p. 98 (Glacier), Dmitry Yashkin p. 98 (mountain bike), Centrill Media p. 103 (annual roundup of the State Park buffalo), Nila Newsom p. 109 (An auto rickshaws driving), 1000 Words p. 112 (A viewer browses Google Play store), Anton Bielousov p. 129 (Andre Luiz Moreira), p. 139 (bottom right), Anton_ Ivanov p. 141 (logo Real Madrid), Marco Iacobucci EPP p. 141 (Real Madrid soccer team), Mehmet Cetin p. 142 (Sales Woman on the souvenir market), Alexey Boldin p. 148 (Google Gmail web page), filmlandscape p. 149 (bottom left), ZRyzner p. 149 (bottom center), Featureflash Photo Agency p. 153 (Surfer Bethany Hamilton), Brian A. Witkin p. 153 (Bethany Hamilton at the Super Girl Pro in Oceanside California), Gustavo Miguel Fernandes p. 153 (Bethany Hamilton in Rip Curl Pro 2010), Twin Design p. 154 (Avatar), Kaspars Grinvalds p. 156 (Netflix on the App Store), Everett Collection p. 157 (Ann Hathaway), Ovidiu Hrubaru p. 157 (Robert de Niro).
Images used under license from © **Shutterstock.com**

© **Wikipedia:** Creative Commons Attribution-Share Alike p. 63, Olav Bjaaland p. 105 (Roald Amundsen y sus compañeros mirando la bandera noruega), Illustreted London News p. 105 (A photograph of a dog team), Henry Bowers p. 105 (Pole party expedition), Abhinav Phangcho Choudhury (http://www.flickr.com/people/60354764@N03) p. 149 (Vagón de tren, India)

# Contents

## Student's Book



## Workbook

# Scope and Sequence



| Unit | Vocabulary | Grammar | Skills |
|---|---|---|---|
| **0** **Who are we?** | **Review:** daily routines, food and drink, free-time activities, transportation<br>**Parts of the Body** | Present simple;<br>*Going to;*<br>*Will;*<br>Time expressions (present and future);<br>Information questions with *wh-* words | **Listening:** Identifying statements and responses |
| **1** **What do you celebrate?** | **Celebrations:** birthday, blow out candles, get a diploma, graduation, Independence Day, make resolutions, New Year's Eve, open presents, set off fireworks, watch a parade, wave flags, wear a cap and gown | Present continuous (future meaning) | **Reading:** Making a mind map<br>**Listening:** Understanding a description of a holiday<br>**Project:** Making a holiday infographic |
| **2** **How are you feeling?** | **First Aid:** antiseptic spray, bandages, burn gel, first-aid kit, ice pack, medicine, thermometer<br>**Symptoms and Injuries:** bruise, cut, fever, headache, runny nose, sore throat, stomachache, sunburn | *Should;*<br>Short answers;<br>Zero conditional | **Listening:** Taking notes to identify main points and supporting examples<br>**Reading:** Reading a magazine article<br>**Project:** Making a fact sheet |
| **3** **How can we save the planet?** | **The Environment:** conserve water, plant trees, pollute the environment, recycle, reduce carbon emissions, save electricity, send garbage to landfills, use clean energy, use fossil fuels | First conditional | **Reading:** Identifying opinions<br>**Writing:** Giving reasons to support your opinions<br>**Project:** Making a minidocumentary |
| **4** **What's your passion?** | **Fan Activities:** be a fan of, be good at, collect action figures, dress up as characters, get an autograph, put on face paint, put up posters, stand in line, wear a hat, wear team colors | Intensifiers;<br>*Already, Yet* | **Reading:** Understanding questions in a dialogue<br>**Speaking:** Asking questions as an active listener<br>**Project:** Making a *Fan Activities* brochure |

| Unit | Vocabulary | Grammar | Skills |
|---|---|---|---|
| 5 How much do you remember? | **Personal Experiences:** buy a lot of souvenirs, fall in love, forget, get in trouble, get lost, have a lot of fun, make a mistake, take care of<br>**Keepsakes:** baby tooth, drawing, necklace, seashell, toy car | Past continuous;<br>Short answers;<br>Past continuous and past simple: *When;*<br>Past continuous: *While* | **Reading:** Making connections between images and text<br>**Listening:** Completing an outline<br>**Project:** Making a personalized timeline |
| 6 What do you need to travel? | **Travel:** book a flight, catch a train, exchange money, get a passport, hire a guide, pack a suitcase, stay in a hotel<br>**Collocations:** get hot, get hungry, get lost, get ready, get started, get there, get thirsty, get up | Present perfect;<br>Short answers;<br>Present perfect: *Ever;*<br>Present perfect: *Already, Yet;*<br>*Been, Gone* | **Reading:** Reading images<br>**Listening:** Identifying images from descriptions<br>**Project:** Making a *Travel Experience* poster |
| 7 How adventurous are you? | **Extreme Sports:** kite surfing, mountain biking, rock climbing, skydiving, snowboarding, white water rafting<br>**Adjectives:** bored, boring, excited, exciting, interested, interesting, terrified, terrifying, thrilled, thrilling, tired, tiring | *Might;*<br>*Would;*<br>Present perfect: *Never* | **Reading:** Understanding text organization<br>**Writing:** Classifying facts<br>**Project:** Making an *Adventure Profile* |
| 8 What do we have in common? | **Habits:** go out to eat, hang out, keep a journal, order take-out, sleep in, stay up late, stream movies, work out | *Too, Either;*<br>*So, Neither;*<br>*Me too, Me neither* | **Listening:** Identifying speakers<br>**Reading:** Reading a blog<br>**Project:** Conducting a *Social Acceptance* survey |

0

# Who are we?

# Unit 0



**1 Look and complete the descriptions of each person.**

0. get up early – always
   yoga ❤
   ride her bike – every day
   bananas
   India

0. Pam always gets up early. She likes to do yoga in the mornings. She rides her bike to school every day. She hates bananas. Her dream is to travel to India in the future.

1. eat breakfast – never
   hang out with friends ❤❤
   walk – always
   carrots and lettuce
   Rio de Janeiro

1. Betty never eat breakfast
   She loves to hang out with friends
   She always Walks
   to school.
   She doesn't like carrots and lettuce
   Her dream is to travel to Rio de Janeiro

2. do homework – sometimes
   drawing ❤
   take a bus – often
   milk
   Italy

2. Ben sometimes do homework.
   He love drawing.
   He often takes bus to school.
   Ben doesn't like milk.
   His dream is to travel to Italy

3. go to the gym – often
   camping ❤❤
   go by car – always
   coffee
   Grand Canyon

3. Tom often go to the gym.
   He love camping.
   He always goes to school by car.
   Tom hates coffee.
   His dream is to go to the Grand Canyon.

## 2 Read and write the name of the person from Activity 1.

0. It's ten o'clock and I'm still in bed. I'm going to get up soon and have breakfast. I'm going to have some coffee to wake up and then I'm going to take a bus to my aunt's house. It's her birthday and I drew a picture for her. Ben

1. I'm here at the gym, but I hate it. I never come, but my mom says I have to exercise. I'm going to eat healthier, too. I always eat junk food. Well, my friends love me the way I am. I'm going to see them again tonight! Betty

2. I'm walking my neighbors' dogs to **make** some **money**. I really want to travel next year. I am going to be ready then. Right now, my parents think I'm too young to travel **abroad** alone, especially to camp alone in the mountains! Tom

3. I know I'm going to be the best instructor in the future! It's so relaxing to do this in my free time. Yes, standing on your head can be relaxing… And it exercises your **willpower**. I'm going to change completely. I'm going to do new things—maybe even eat bananas! Ram

## 3 Listen and number the photos.

0

## 4 Listen again and match.

0. It's cold in here.
1. What does your new dress look like?
2. The school called. Robby is sick.
3. Mandy's birthday is tomorrow.
4. Grandma is lonely.
5. It's a good movie.

- I'll bake her a cake.
- I'll pick him up.
- I'll try to see it on the weekend.
- I'll visit her this afternoon.
- I'll draw it for you.
- I'll close the window.

### Guess What!

We use *will* to express immediate reactions to comments:

This bag is very heavy.
I **will** carry it for you.

### Glossary

**make money:** earn money
**abroad:** a foreign country
**willpower:** determination and self-control

**5** **Look at the pictures and circle the main differences in their appearance.**

**6** **Read the text and check. Then label the body parts.**

Humans' closest relatives, the Neanderthals, lived in Europe and Asia during the Ice Age, about 200,000 to 30,000 years ago. They looked similar to us, but there were some differences in their
10 **appearance**. They were shorter and more muscular than modern humans. This short and **stocky** stature was ideal for the cold weather because it consolidated heat. You can learn a lot about their activities just by looking at the remains of bones. One interesting thing is that their **arms** were **asymmetrical**: one arm was always stronger than the other, usually the right one. One of the possible reasons for this is that they spent a lot of time **scraping** animal skins, an activity that involves a lot of muscle work. Neanderthals also had really strong **hands**, ready to hunt and work. Their **legs** were short and strong and their **feet** quite big, which suggests that they walked and ran a lot. They were much more active than we are!

Neanderthals had flatter **heads** than us, but their **brains** were large, not small as many people thought. They had prominent **brow ridges** and their **cheekbones** were more angular. They had wider **noses** than humans and most Neanderthals had light **skin**. There is evidence that some Neanderthals had red **hair** and even **freckles**!

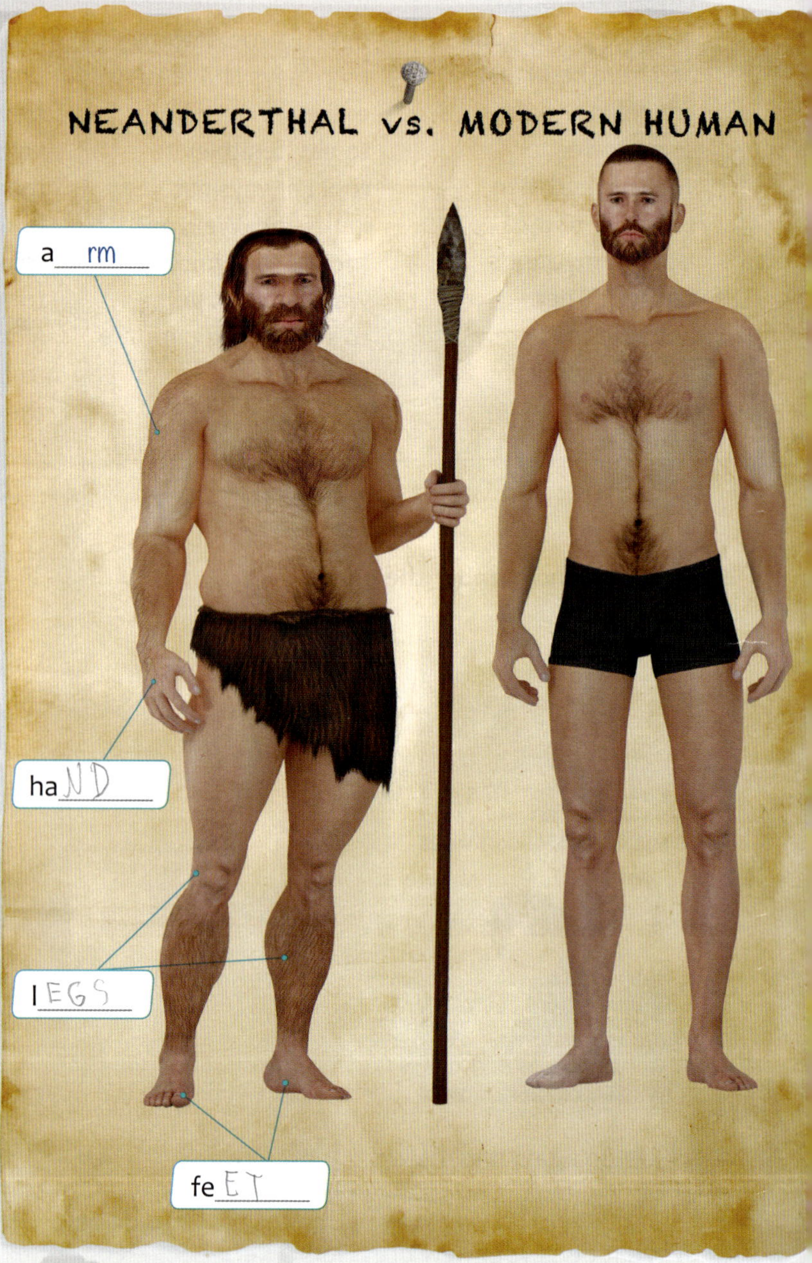


**7** **Read again and match the questions and answers.**

0. Where did the Neanderthals live?
1. When did they live there?
2. Did they look similar to modern humans?
3. Why were they short and stocky?
4. Were their brains smaller than ours?

No, they weren't.
Yes, they did.
In Europe and Asia.
Because they needed more heat.
During the Ice Age.

**Glossary**

**appearance:** the way that someone or something looks

**stocky:** short and heavy; compact

**asymmetrical:** having two sides that are not the same; not symmetrical

**scraping:** removing (something) from a surface by rubbing an object or tool against it

**8** Listen and circle the verbs you can hear.

**9** Complete the sentences using the verbs from Activity 8.

0. Neanderthals ______ used ______ sophisticated tools.
1. They ____________ on cave walls.
2. They ____________ their relatives in sickness.
3. Neanderthals ____________ their dead.
4. They ____________ music, too.

3 min **10 Think Fast!** Change the sentences in Activity 9 into questions.

0. What did Neanderthals use ____________?
1. Where ____________?
2. Who ____________?
3. What ____________?
4. Did ____________?

**Guess What!**

One of the most surprising facts is that Neanderthals lived in Europe and Asia before humans. Neanderthals and humans both originated on the African continent, and scientists believe that for a period of time they both lived on Earth at the same time.

# 1 What do you celebrate?

# Vocabulary



**1 Look at Lisa's scrapbook page and label the events.**

Matt's graduation | Anna's birthday | Independence Day | New Year's Eve

**2 Read and number the photo captions.**

___ My cousin's **blowing out** her **candles**! I can't believe she's ten!

___ He's **wearing a cap and gown**. He looks really **handsome**.

___ We're **watching a parade**! This marching band is playing the **national anthem**.

___ She's **opening** her **presents**! That one was from me!

___ Here he's **getting a diploma**! He starts **college** in the fall.

___ Everyone's **waving** American **flags** and wearing red, white and blue!

___ I'm **making resolutions**. Next year, I want to eat better and smile more!

___ They're **setting off** fireworks. Beautiful!

**3 Read and complete the celebration activities.**

1. make ____________
2. blow out ____________
3. wear a ____________
4. set off ____________
5. wave ____________
6. open ____________
7. get a ____________
8. watch a ____________

**4 [3] Listen and number the celebrations.**

Independence Day ☐ a birthday ☐ New Year's Eve ☐ graduation ☐

**5 Classify the words.**

cake candles cap and gown fireworks flag diploma marching band parade presents singing

| Independence Day | Birthday | New Year's Eve | Graduation |
|---|---|---|---|
| | | | |

**Guess What!**
On New Year's Eve in Denmark, people **smash** plates against their friends' doors for good luck in the next year.

**Glossary**

**handsome:** good-looking

**national anthem:** the official song of a country

**college:** a school where you go after high school to get a bachelor's degree

**smash:** to break

3 min **6 Think Fast!** Scramble five celebrations words for a classmate to guess.

# Grammar

Every year, millions of people celebrate Thanksgiving by watching the Macy's Thanksgiving day parade in New York City.

**1 Read quickly and complete.**

16 Thanksgiving is one of the largest celebrations in the United States. It is always on the fourth Thursday of November. Millions of people gather for a day of feasting, football and family. On Thanksgiving morning, 3.5 million people watch the Macy's Thanksgiving Day Parade in New York City. More than 50 million people watch the event on TV. In the afternoon or evening, families have a delicious turkey dinner.

**2 Read and circle the correct option.**

1. Thanksgiving is **today** / **next week.**
2. They **are** / **aren't** celebrating Thanksgiving in New York.
3. They **are** / **aren't** visiting their grandparents next week.

**Guess What!**
Pumpkin pie is the most popular pie for Thanksgiving dinners.

**Present Continuous (future meaning)**

We can use Present Continuous to talk about future plans, such as a travel itinerary.

## 3 Listen and mark (✓ or ✗) the plans for the trip.

| | |
|---|---|
| flying ✗ | taking the bus ✓ |
| staying in a hotel ✗ | staying with their grandparents ✓ |
| having dinner ✓ | watching football ✓ |
| going shopping at midnight ✗ | going to the parade ✓ |

## 4 Listen and circle *T* (True) or *F* (False).

1. The kids are arriving tomorrow morning. T (F)
2. Grandma is baking a pie this afternoon. T (F)
3. She's cooking the turkey on Thursday. (T) F
4. Grandpa isn't helping with the preparations. (T) F
5. He's taking the grandkids to the parade. (T) F

## 5 Listen again and unscramble the sentences.

1. are / when / coming / the kids
   When are kids coming?
2. not / I / making / a pie / am
   I am not making a pie.
3. you / taking / the kids / to / are / the parade
   are you taking the kids to the parade
4. cooking / the turkey / on Thursday / am / I
   I am cooking the turkey on. thursday

3 min **6 Think Fast!** In your notebook, write five sentences about Stickman's plans for Thanksgiving.

**Glossary**

**bakery:** a store where you can buy bread, cake, cookies or pies

**nap:** a short sleep during the day

# Reading & Listening

**1 Read and circle the correct option.**

## Religious Celebrations

All over the world, religious celebrations are important to billions of people! Here are two religious celebrations: bar and bat mitzvahs and Eid al-Fitr.

### Bar and Bat Mitzvahs

18

In the Jewish community, a boy becomes a bar mitzvah when he turns 13. (A bat mitzvah is a similar ceremony for girls when they turn 12.) This event celebrates the transition to **adulthood**. As a part of the occasion, children **recite** religious texts. After this ceremony, the bar or bat mitzvah receives gifts and money in multiples of 18—a number that symbolizes a long life. From this time on, they can participate as adults in religious activities.

### Eid al-Fitr

Eid al-Fitr (pronounced ed œl fIt-Ur) is an important religious holiday for the world's two billion Muslims. Eid al-Fitr, or Eid, is the first day after Ramadan, a month of **fasting**. On this day, Muslims say **prayers** and have a special meal. Children open presents. Many people give to the poor or donate money to charities, an important part of the religion.

1. Bar and bat mitzvahs are **Jewish** / **Muslim** celebrations.
2. A *bar mitzvah* is the name of a celebration and the **boy** / **girl** who participates.
3. In a bat mitzvah, the participant is **12** / **13**.
4. The number **12** / **18** represents long life.
5. Eid al-Fitr is a **Jewish** / **Muslim** celebration.
6. Eid occurs **before** / **after** Ramadan.
7. People celebrate Eid by **fasting** / **eating**.

**Be Strategic!**
Making a mind map can help you to understand and remember information from a text. Identify the topics and then add details.

**2 Read again and complete the mind map in your notebook.**

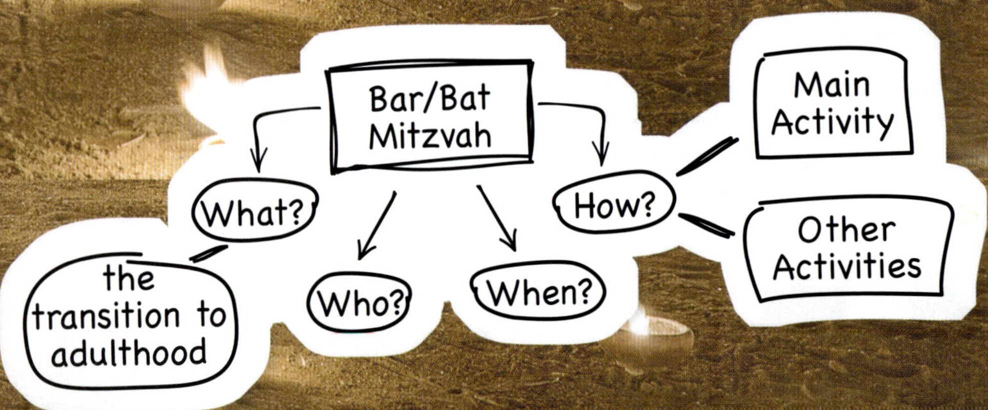


**Glossary**

**adulthood:** being an adult

**recite:** to read a text aloud

**fasting:** living without food or drink

**prayers:** requests or expressions of gratitude

**3** Listen and number. 6

Wesak is a religious celebration, so many Buddhists go to a temple to pray and meditate. They often take flowers and __________ with them. ☐

And in general, when we celebrate Wesak Day, we try to make other people __________, especially people who are poor or sick. ☐

Sunisa here! It's May and next week is a very special holiday in Thailand, and for Buddhists all over the __________: Wesak Day! On Wesak, we celebrate the **birth**, the **enlightenment** and the **death** of Buddha. ☐

At the temple, people give __________ to the Buddhist monks—men who devote themselves to a simple life (they're easy to identify because they wear **robes**). At night, everyone walks around the temple __________ times in a special ceremony. ☐

**4** Listen again and complete. 6

**5** In your notebook, make a mind map for Wesak Day.

**Stop and Think!** What do you know about religious celebrations around the world?

**Glossary**

**birth:** when a person is born

**enlightenment:** spiritual awakening

**death:** when a person dies

**robes:** long, loose gowns

# Culture

**1 Read the facts about Mexico and underline the one you find the most interesting.**

## Did you know...

In 2015, nearly 26 million tourists visited Mexico.

The smallest dog **breed** in the world, the chihuahua, got its name after the State of Chihuahua in northern Mexico.

Mexico has 11 active volcanoes.

Every year, millions of monarch butterflies travel to Mexico from the US and Canada.

The largest pyramid in the world is in Cholula, in the Mexican state of Puebla.

There are 32 UNESCO world heritage sites in Mexico.

Foods like red tomato, corn, avocado and chocolate originated in Mexico.

**2 Read and label.**

Why? Who? When? Main Activities Other Activities

When

November 1st and 2nd

Who

people in Mexico: families, schools

Why

to remember to people who have died

Main activities

creating an *ofrenda*: a display with *pan de muerto*—"bread of the dead," sugar skulls, candles and flowers

Other activities

R.I.P.

visiting **graves** in a **cemetery** (Some people stay all night!)

decorating homes and public spaces with *calacas*

# LA CATRINA

*La Catrina* is one of the most popular symbols of the Day of the Dead in Mexico. What is *La Catrina*? It's a skeleton of a woman in an elegant hat and a long formal dress.

La Catrina is the invention of a famous Mexican illustrator, Jose Guadalupe Posada, just before the Mexican Revolution. He drew La Catrina in 1910 to make fun of **wealthy** Mexicans who imitated European styles. Posada took his inspiration from Mictecacihuatl (mIk-tEk-si-wa-t´l), the Aztec goddess of death and queen of the underworld. Posada only illustrated the head of La Catrina in 1910. In 1947, the Mexican artist Diego Rivera painted a full-length view of La Catrina in the mural *"Dream of a Sunday Afternoon in Alameda Park."*

Nowadays, some people wear costumes to look like La Catrina, even outside of Mexico.

▲ *La Catrina*, by Jose Guadalupe Posada

**3 Read and answer in your notebook.**

1. What is *La Catrina*?
2. When did Jose Guadalupe Posada invent this figure?
3. Why did he draw this figure wearing an elegant hat?
4. Who is Mictecacihuatl?
5. How was Diego Rivera's Catrina different?

**Stop and Think!** How can holidays bring people together as a community?

**Glossary**

**breed:** a type of dog with specific characteristics

**graves:** tombs; spaces for dead people in a cemetery

**cemetery:** an area with tombs

**wealthy:** rich

# Project

**1 Look at the St. Patrick's Day infographic on page 23. Read and match.**

1. St. Patrick is the patron of this country.
2. This plant is a symbol of Ireland.
3. This is a common Irish surname.
4. The first St. Patrick's Day parade was here.
5. These are Irish instruments.
6. This is a magical creature.
7. People celebrate St. Patrick's Day here too.

- Murphy
- Boston
- leprechaun
- Ireland
- Australia
- shamrock
- bagpipes

**2 7 Listen and complete the sentences.**

1. Shaun's surname is ______.
2. He lives in ______.
3. His family is originally from ______.
4. There's a big ______ and fireworks in Sydney on St. Patrick's Day.
5. This year his family is having a ______ with Irish music and dancing.

**3 Choose and research another celebration's origins and traditions.**

Halloween

Hanukkah

Groundhog Day

Mardi Gras

Easter

Memorial Day

**4 Make an infographic with your findings. Add a party invitation to your infographic.**

# Happy St. Patrick's Day

17 March

St. Patrick's Day is March 17. According to tradition, this is the date of St. Patrick's death.

| 387 | 403 | 409 | 432 | 461 |
|---|---|---|---|---|
| Patrick was born in Roman England. | Pirates kidnapped Patrick and took him to Ireland as a slave. | Patrick escaped and returned to England. | Patrick went to Ireland to teach Christianity. | Patrick died. |



The shamrock—a common three-leafed plant in Ireland—is a symbol of Ireland and St. Patrick's Day. St. Patrick used the shamrock to teach about his religion.

St. Patrick's Day is special to people with Irish ancestors. Common Irish surnames include Murphy, Kelly, O'Brien, Ryan, O'Neill and O'Connor.

The very first St. Patrick's Day parade was not in Ireland but in Boston in **1737.**

Even people in Australia celebrate St. Patrick's Day!

St. Patrick's Day parades normally include people playing bagpipes, a traditional Irish instrument.

**90%** of Americans celebrate St. Patrick's Day! In the US, you can buy green "shamrock" milkshakes on St. Patrick's Day. In Chicago, they dye the river green to celebrate this day.

Many people dress as leprechauns for St. Patrick's Day. A leprechaun is a kind of magical creature: a little man with a beard dressed in green clothing.

# Review

**1 Look and label the celebrations.**

1 

______________

2 

______________

3 

______________

4 

______________

**2 Read and match. Then look and number the scenes.**

1. blow out
2. get

a cap and gown
candles
a parade

3. set off
4. make

flags
a diploma
fireworks
presents

6. watch
resolutions
5. wear

7. wave
8. open

## 3 Unscramble the sentences.

1. you / what / doing / after / school / are / ?

______________________________

2. is / Janice / party / not / going / the / to

______________________________

3. we / giving / sweater / for / Tim / birthday / a / his / are

______________________________

4. to / you / the / going / football / are / tonight / game / ?

______________________________

5. parents / are / my / having / not / for / Thanksgiving / turkey

______________________________



## 4 Complete the e-mail using the correct forms of the verbs.

New Message

File Edit View Insert Format Tools Message Help

Send

From: giovanni.pizoli@avsd.net

To: jess.robinson@avsd.net

Arial 10

Hi Jessica,

Are (1) ____________ (*have*) a nice summer? I'm in Rome with my Italian cousins. It's a lot of fun! Tomorrow, we (2) ____________ (*go*) to the Colosseum and then we (3) ____________ (*have*) lunch in Piazza Navona. Pizza, pizza and more pizza! Later, my mom (4) ____________ (*go*) shopping with my aunt, but I (5) ____________ (*take*) a tour of the Vatican. Yes, I love sightseeing 🙂!
We (6) ____________ (*not visit*) any other museums because we don't have time, but we (7) ____________ (*take*) a bus to see an ancient Roman villa on Friday. And we (8) ____________ (*travel*) back home next week. I'll text you!

Ciao from Rome,

Giovanni

## 5 Rewrite the sentences.

1. We're going to a rock concert tonight! → ?

______________________________

2. My friend Amy's going to the parade. → –

______________________________

3. We aren't setting off fireworks tonight. → +

______________________________

4. Is Paul having a graduation party? → +

______________________________

5. You're going to the party. → ?

______________________________

# Just for Fun

**1 Read and guess the holiday. Unscramble and write.**

**1 EWHALONLE**

_______________________

**2 EANDPENDIDEN YCE**

_______________________

**3 ANEENYLTI'A DVS**

_______________________

**4 VIKINGSHANTG**

_______________________

**2 Read and solve the puzzle.**

**Down**

1. a skeleton in a dress
2. lights on a birthday cake
3. a popular food on Thanksgiving
4. gifts people receive

**Across**

5. a document you receive at graduation
6. a square hat for graduation
7. decisions for the New Year
8. holidays or special occasions

**Guess What!**

Finland has a wife-carrying festival! It's a race! Husbands carry their wives through a 235-meter obstacle course.

2

# How are you feeling?

# Vocabulary



1 [8] Listen and number the items.

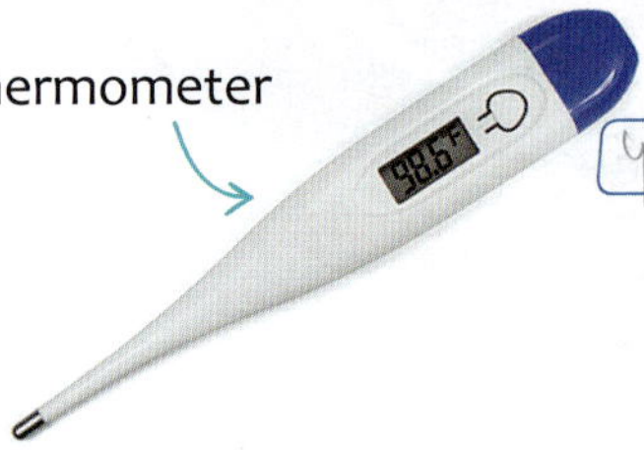
thermometer — 4

bandages — 2

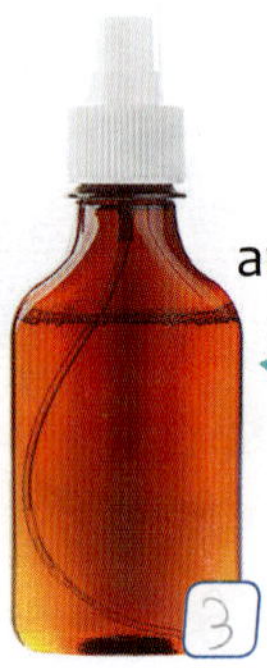
antiseptic spray — 3

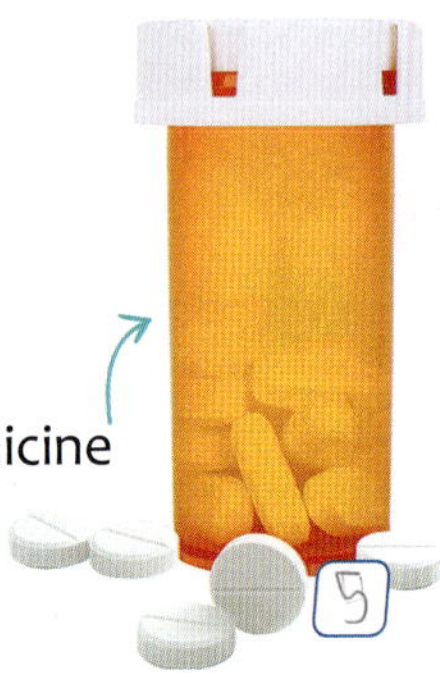
medicine — 5

burn gel — 6

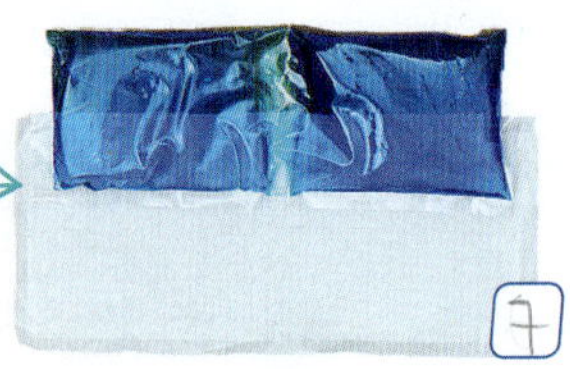
ice pack — 7

first-aid kit — 1

2 Read the comic and label the symptoms and injuries.

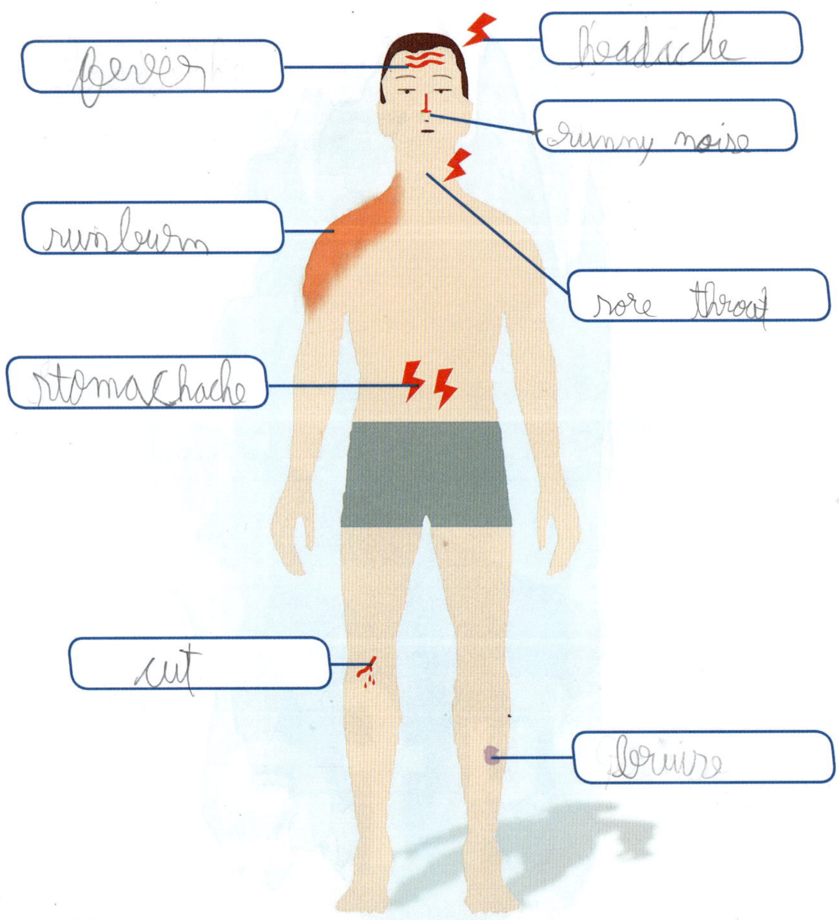

**3** Look and suggest what to use in each case.

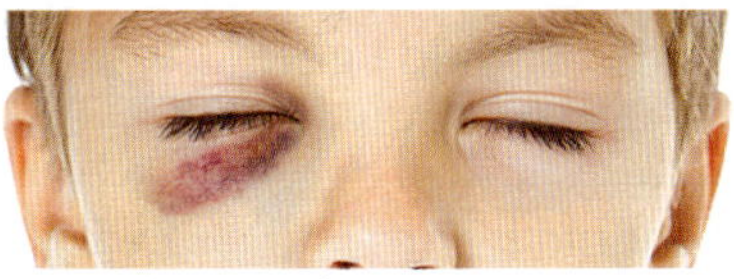

ice pack

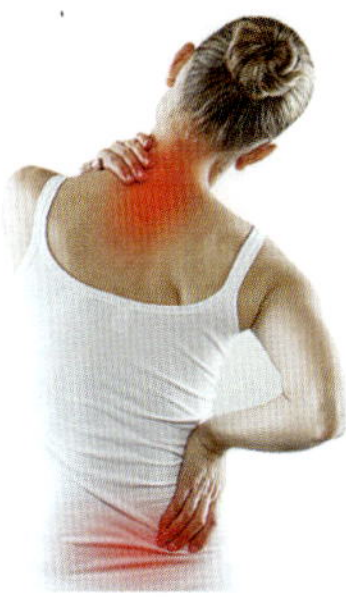

medicine

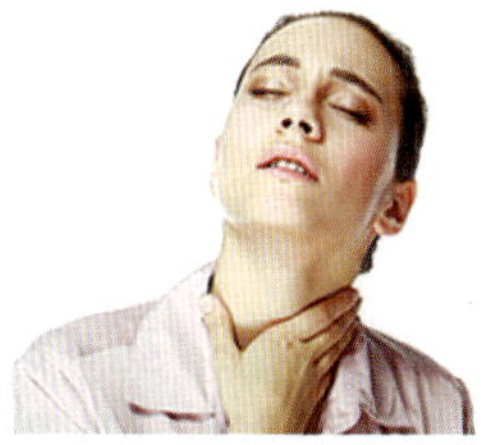

medicine

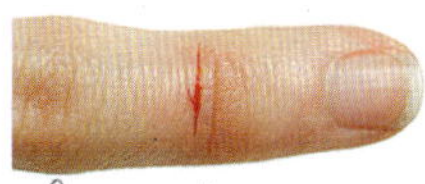

bandage

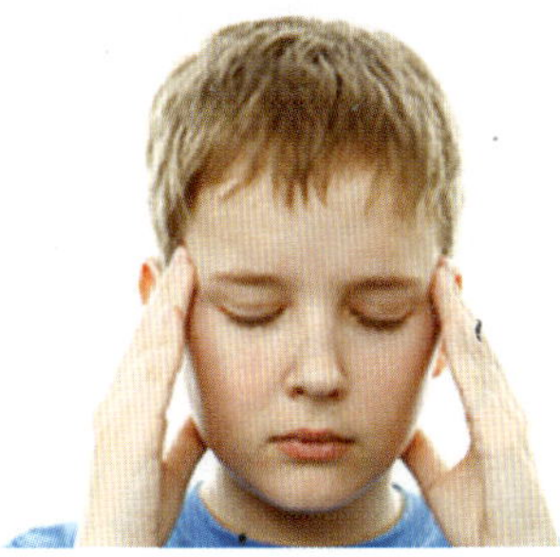

medicine

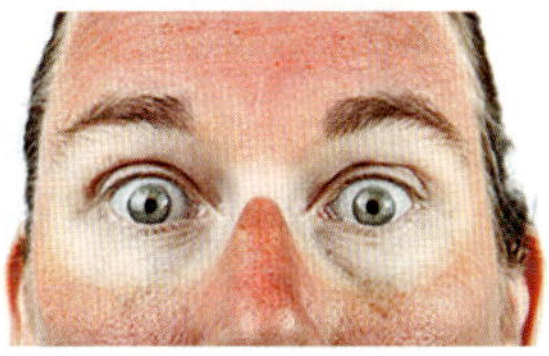

burn gel

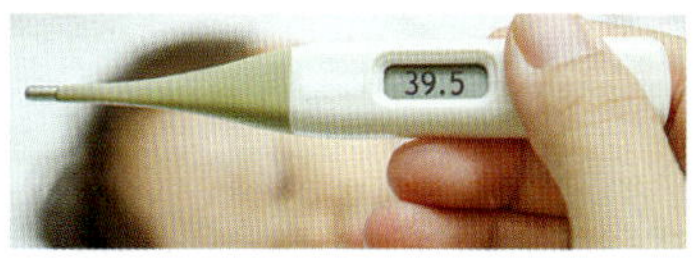


medicine

3 min **4 Think Fast!** Write two examples for each category in your notebook.

Symptoms Injuries First Aid

# Grammar

**1 Rate the health factors. How do they affect a person's health?**

1. exercising
2. smoking cigarettes
3. drinking soda
4. going to bed late
5. being stressed out
6. listening to loud music
7. eating a balanced diet
8. reducing screen time

30

**2 9 Listen and number the recommendations.**

- wear a seatbelt
- turn down the volume
- wear a helmet
- get enough sleep

**3 Look and answer with a classmate.**

- Is it OK to drink soda?
- How much sleep should I get?
- Should I stop checking Facebook in bed?
- What should I include in my diet?
- What kind of exercise should I do?
- How much water should I drink?

### Should

We use *should* for advice and recommendations:
You **should** exercise junk food.
You **shouldn't** eat junk food.

### Guess What!

We often use *you* to talk about people in general: **You** shouldn't eat cake for breakfast.

## Zero Conditional

These sentences express facts using Present Simple. You can use *if* or *when* to express the condition.

**4 Read the sentences. Circle the conditions and then underline the consequences.**

1. When you reduce your screen time, you have more time for other activities.
2. You can avoid many health problems if you eat a balanced diet.

**5 Read the examples in Activity 4. Then circle *T* (True) or *F* (False).**

1. The condition always comes before the consequence. T F
2. *If* and *when* have the same meaning in conditionals. T F
3. You need a comma (,) after the consequence. T F
4. You use the Present Simple in the condition. T F
5. You use the Present Simple in the consequence. T F

**6 Complete the sentences.**

1. you drink water / your digestion is better
   When you drink water.
2. you don't sleep enough / you feel terrible
   If you don't sleep enough you feel terrible.
3. you look at a screen too long / you can't fall asleep
   When you look at a screen to long you can't fall asleep.
4. you eat well / you feel better
   If you eat well you feel better.

3 min **7 Think Fast!** **In your notebook, rewrite the sentences in Activity 6. Put the consequence first in each sentence.**

# Listening and Reading

**1 Look and discuss with a classmate. What makes you happy?**

- caring about others ☐
- good food ☐
- money ☐
- community ☐
- exercise ☐
- sunshine ☐
- music ☐
- pets ☐
- relaxation ☐
- positive thinking ☐



**Be Strategic!**
Taking notes can help you to distinguish between main points and supporting examples.

**2** [10] **Listen and mark (✓) the topics you hear.**

**3** [10] **Listen again and add the topics from Activity 2 to the chart. Then complete the examples.**

| Happiness Factors | Examples |
|---|---|
| 1. | ______, ______, **strangers** |
| 2. | ______, gratitude and kindness |
| 3. | going to the gym, playing ______ or taking a ______ |
| 4. | a ______, a ______, a ______ |
| 5. | going to a **festival**, joining a ______, ______ |

**Guess What!**
According to the United Nation's World Happiness Report, Denmark is the happiest country in the world followed by Norway, Switzerland and the Netherlands.

**4 Read and choose the best option.**

The article explains how to be kind and optimistic. ☐

The article explains how to focus on the present moment. ☒

The article gives a few techniques for relaxation. ☐

# How **mindful** are you?

Breathe in… Breathe out… Focus only on your breathing…. Breathe in… Breathe out… But your mind is somewhere else! You're thinking about a test… or an argument with a friend. You're wondering if you have any messages. Maybe you're hungry for a snack or imagining your afternoon routine. LOTS of things can distract us—**regrets** about the past or **worries** about the future—and we forget to see and feel and listen. Mindfulness is the opposite of that.

When you're mindful, you actively focus on the present moment. Mindfulness is experiencing the world in high definition! What is your body doing? What are your thoughts? What is happening around you? And when you're mindful, you suspend criticism. Be aware of your thoughts. Observe them.

"Mindfulness" has its origins in ancient Buddhism, but it isn't necessary to be Buddhist to practice mindfulness. In fact, many schools offer classes in mindfulness and meditation. It improves your health and memory. It reduces stress, too. Do you want to try it? Here's a technique to practice: Observe a raisin. Look at it carefully. Look at every detail. How does it feel in your hand? **Notice** its weight. Try to observe everything about the raisin. Then eat the raisin as slowly as possible. What do you notice? What sensations do you experience?

Now, imagine if you eat everything in this way. Imagine that in a conversation, you notice the details in a person's expression. Every time you go outside, you feel the air touch your face and notice the sound of your footsteps. It is a simple exercise, but it can improve your life!

33

**5 Read again and complete.**

1. Mindfulness focuses on the ____________________.
2. ____________________ often distract us from noticing the world around us.
3. One of the techniques to stay mindful is to ____________________.
4. Mindfulness can improve ____________________ and ____________________.

**Stop and Think!** How can being mindful help you be happy?

## Glossary

**strangers:** people you don't know

**festival:** a community celebration

**regrets:** negative feelings about the past; guilt

**worries:** (sing. worry) anxiety about the future

**notice:** see; pay attention to

# Culture



**1 Read and circle the correct option. Then check the answers below.**

1. There are ____________ countries in Africa.
   a) 14
   b) 42
   c) 54
2. The most common language in Africa is ____________
   a) English.
   b) Arabic.
   c) Swahili.
3. The largest city in Africa is ____________
   a) Johannesburg, South Africa.
   b) Cairo, Egypt.
   c) Lagos, Nigeria.
4. In 1967, the first heart **transplant** took place in ____________
   a) Kenya.
   b) South Africa.
   c) Nigeria.
5. Rhinos are in danger because people in ____________ believe that their horns have medicinal properties.
   a) America
   b) Europe
   c) Asia

Answers: 1. 54, 2. English, 3. Lagos, 4. South Africa, 5. Asia

**2 Read and number.**

1. A Traditional African Medicine
2. Traditional **Healers**
3. **Healthcare** in Africa
4. Healers and Modern Medicine

In Africa, healthcare comes in many forms. There are doctors and hospitals to treat major illnesses, but in some countries, there is only one doctor for every 50,000 people! This is one reason that many Africans use traditional medicine.

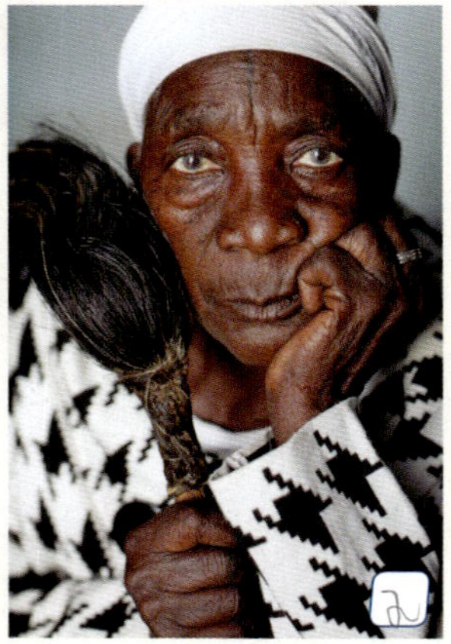

People also consult traditional healers who use special plants, animal parts or minerals as medicine. Sometimes they treat people by doing dances. Many people trust healers more than doctors.

In some parts of Africa, a plant called *buchu* is a popular medicine. It can treat infections. People sometimes use the leaves to make tea.

Some healers also have **training** in modern medicine. They can identify symptoms of diseases such as tuberculosis and HIV/AIDS. Healers can send people with these **diseases** to a doctor to get medication.

## 3 Read again and match.

1. Traditional medicine
2. Some countries
3. *Buchu*
4. Healers use
5. Some healers learn
6. Tuberculosis and HIV/AIDS

- is a medicinal plant.
- modern medicine.
- is very common.
- are diseases.
- plants, animal parts or minerals.
- have few doctors.

## 4 11 Listen and circle *T* (True) or *F* (False).

1. Blessing Kwomo is a doctor. T F
2. She is from South Africa. T F
3. The De Rehoboths Therapeutic Studio helps families prevent diseases. T F
4. They provide transportation to clinics and hospitals. T F
5. They provide medical treatment and health education. T F
6. They give money to the patients. T F

**Stop and Think!** What do you do to stay healthy?

## 5 11 Listen again and complete.

**Problem:** Patients get sick again after treatment.

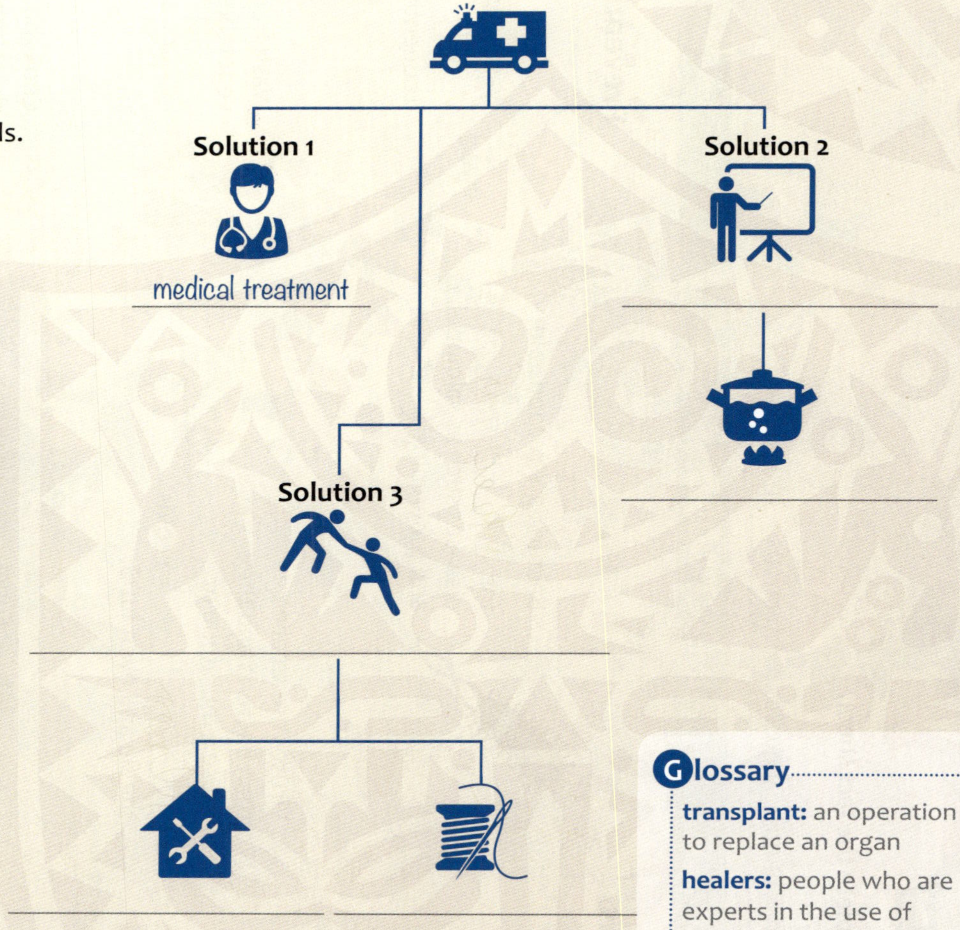


**Glossary**

**transplant:** an operation to replace an organ

**healers:** people who are experts in the use of traditional medicine

**healthcare:** medical care

**training:** instruction

**diseases:** severe illnesses

**entrepreneur:** a person who starts a business

# Project

**1 Read and complete the fact sheet.**

cause clean hands illnesses infectious transmitted

## INFECTIOUS DISEASES

### Symptoms

fever

diarrhea

muscle pain

coughing

### Causes

Bacteria are responsible for ______________ diseases such as salmonella and tuberculosis.

Viruses are smaller than bacteria and they cause a multitude of ______________: colds, the flu and even AIDS.

Fungi ______________ skin diseases, such as athlete's foot. Fungi can also infect your lungs or nervous system.

Parasites cause many diseases. Malaria is caused by a parasite that is ______________ by mosquitoes.

### Prevention

Wash your ______________ frequently.

Wash fruits and vegetables.

Cook food thoroughly.

Drink ______________ water.

Get vaccinations.

**2 Read the fact sheet about Chikungunya on page 37. Then answer the questions.**

1. What are the symptoms of Chikungunya?
______________
2. What causes the disease?
______________
3. How can you prevent it?
______________

**3 Make a fact sheet about an infectious disease.**

1. Include sections for symptoms, causes and prevention.
2. Include other important facts: countries, number of cases, etc.

# CHIKUNGUNYA

## CAUSES

What **causes** Chikungunya?
Chikungunya is caused by **a virus**.

**Mosquitoes** transmit this virus.

It is present in **45** countries.

It affects **1.7 million** people.



## SYMPTOMS

Chikungunya is characterized by fever and pain in the joints. Other symptoms may include headache, muscle pain, joint swelling or a rash.

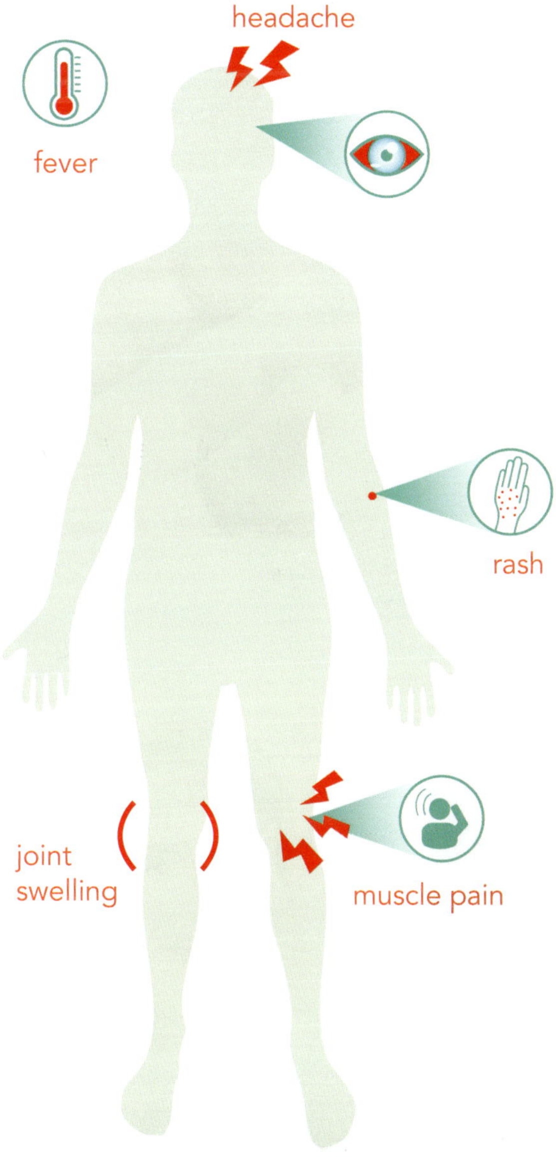


## PREVENTION

There is **no** vaccine for Chikungunya.

You prevent Chikungunya by preventing **mosquito** bites.

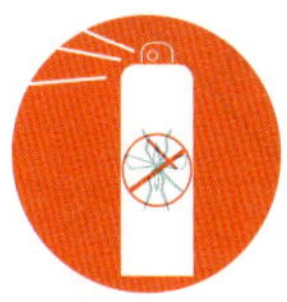

Use mosquito repellant.

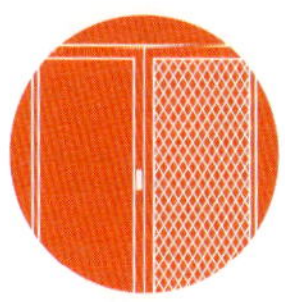

Use mosquito nets.

Empty water containers where mosquitoes reproduce.

In some regions, people prevent Chikungunya by having a pet fish in their water containers. The fish eats the mosquito larvae and prevents the transmission of diseases!

# Review

**1 Read and match.**

1. antiseptic spray
2. burn gel
3. bandages
4. first aid kit
5. ice pack
6. medicine
7. thermometer

- a substance for skin damage caused by the sun or something hot
- something you take to treat an illness
- a very cold bag to put on an injury
- an instrument for measuring temperature
- a substance for preventing infection
- a box or bag containing medicines, creams and bandages
- a strip of cloth or plastic to cover an injury

**2 Find and circle eight words for symptoms and injuries.**

38

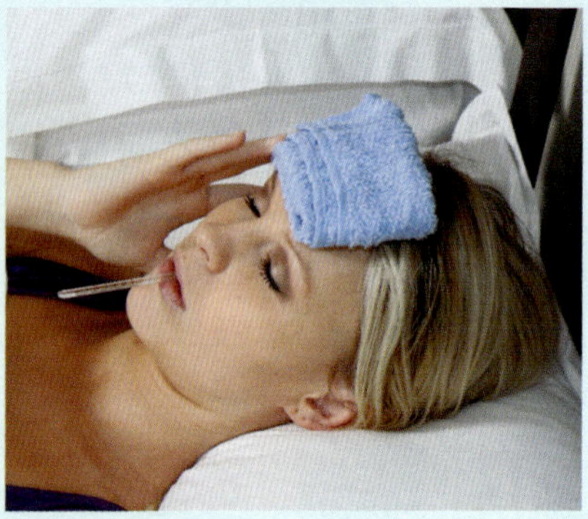
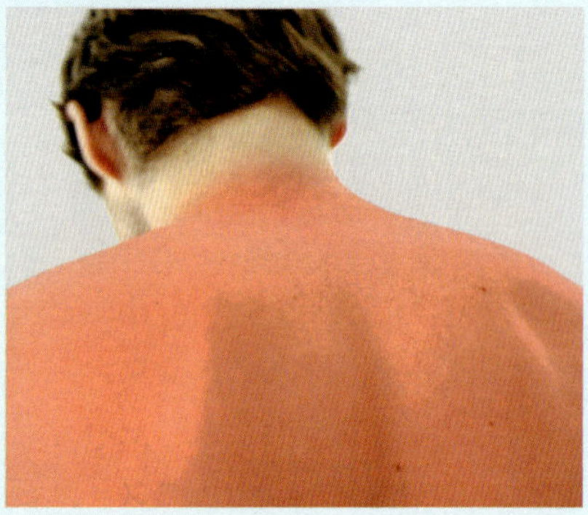

| I | F | C | B | P | B | H | I | E | T | B | W | T |
|---|---|---|---|---|---|---|---|---|---|---|---|---|
| L | I | E | Q | R | R | I | J | A | R | E | E | E |
| N | M | G | U | O | K | M | O | K | T | C | H | U |
| B | D | I | H | E | C | R | O | U | U | J | C | U |
| Y | S | A | U | Z | H | R | E | V | E | F | A | S |
| E | A | B | E | T | C | Q | O | Z | F | E | H | U |
| H | U | Y | E | C | G | A | K | P | Q | O | C | N |
| D | E | R | U | N | N | Y | N | O | S | E | A | B |
| D | O | A | E | C | F | N | K | J | W | J | M | U |
| S | S | U | D | B | T | M | O | Y | T | H | O | R |
| F | T | E | I | A | L | U | C | E | J | E | T | N |
| O | G | X | V | V | C | H | C | M | F | N | S | U |
| T | E | C | E | S | J | H | R | F | O | K | E | F |
| K | R | R | X | J | V | L | E | B | R | T | J | P |

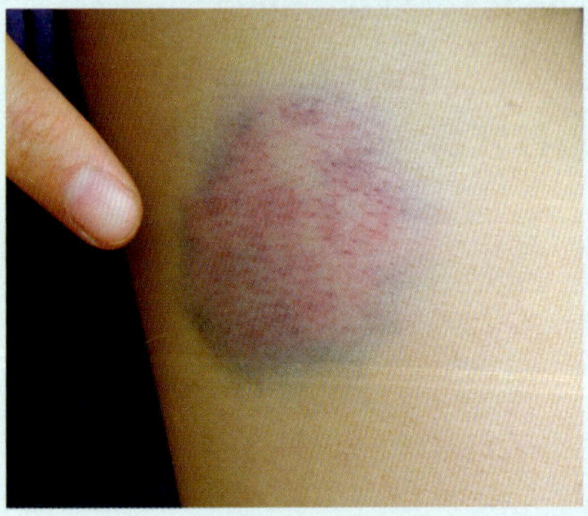
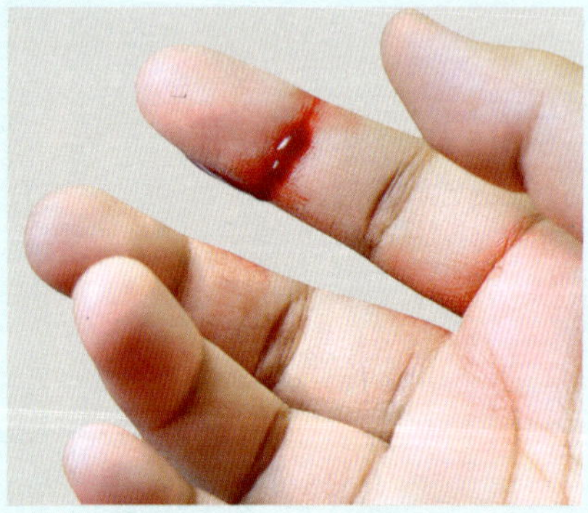

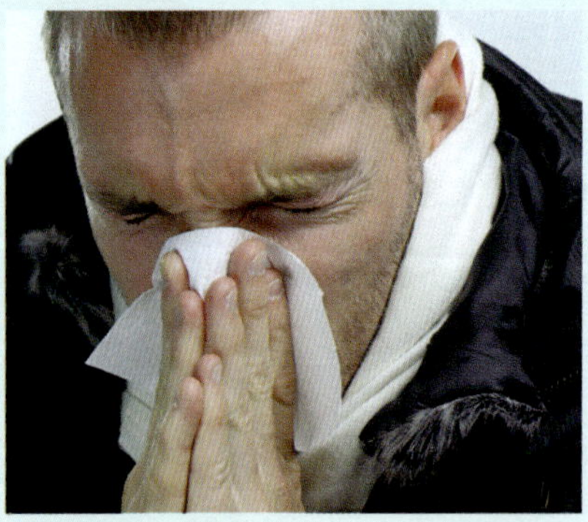

## 3 Write sentences using *should* and *shouldn't.*

1 eat candy for breakfast

3 exercise regularly

2 brush your teeth after every meal

4 watch TV for six hours every day

1. you shouldn't eat candy for breakfast
2. you should brush your teeth after every meal
3. you should exercise regularly
4. you shouldn't watch tv for six hours every day

## 4 Read and underline the consequence.

1. If you eat more vegetables, you reduce your risk of disease.
2. It's easier to lose weight if you stop drinking soda.
3. When you meditate, you forget about worries and regrets.
4. People are happier when they practice positive thinking.

## 5 Correct the sentences.

1. You gain weight when you to consume a lot of calories.
2. When you burn calories, you exercise.
   When you exercise you burn calories
3. When you're breaking a bone, it takes six weeks to heal.
4. If you didn't drink enough water, you become dehydrated.
   don't
5. If you get sick, you don't wash your hands regularly.
   If you don't wash your hands regularly you get sick

# Just for Fun



**1 Take the trivia quiz. Read and circle *T* (True) or *F* (False). Then check your answers on page 158.**

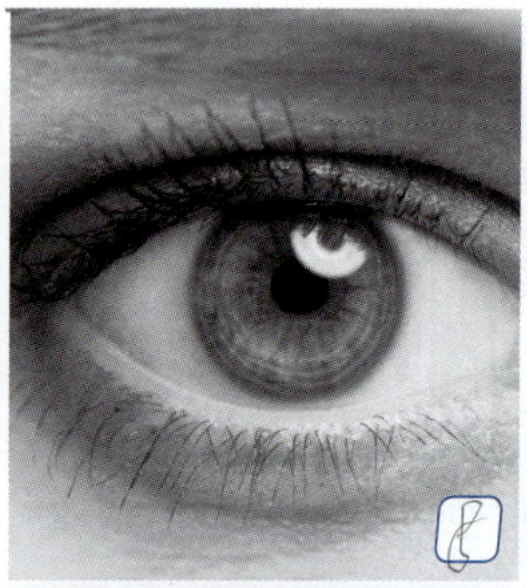

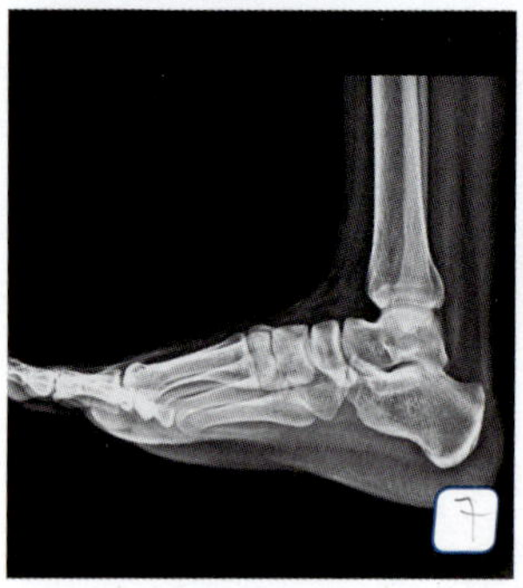

| | | |
|---|---|---|
| 1. It takes 20 minutes of walking to burn the calories in a candy bar. | T | F |
| 2. Laughing can strengthen the immune system. | T | F |
| 3. The human body is more than 60% water. | T | F |
| 4. You don't burn calories when you sleep. | T | F |
| 5. You share 75% of your DNA with a banana. | T | F |
| 6. It takes 18 hours to digest fruits and vegetables. | T | F |
| 7. About 20% of your bones are in your feet. | T | F |
| 8. You blink 28,000 times per day. | T | F |

**2 Read again and number the photos. Then underline the fact that surprised you the most.**

**3 Read the proverbs. Do you agree?**

Early to bed, early to rise makes a man healthy, wealthy and wise.

Seven days without exercise makes one weak.

An apple a day keeps the doctor away.

You are what you eat.

Prevention is better than cure.

Health is wealth.

# 3

# How can we save the planet?

# Vocabulary



### Know Your Footprint
Carbon dioxide, or $CO_2$, is a gas in our atmosphere. Too much $CO_2$ can cause severe changes in our planet's climate! **Reduce carbon emissions** today!

### Use Less Fuel
Most vehicles **use fossil fuels** and produce a lot of $CO_2$. Take the bus or **carpool**—it's more efficient!

### Conserve Water
Take short showers and don't use more water than necessary.

### Save Electricity
Most **power plants** generate electricity using fossil fuels. Save electricity by turning off lights and appliances when you aren't using them.

### Plant Trees
Trees absorb carbon dioxide, protect the **soil** and keep temperatures cooler in the summer. Plant one today!

### Use Clean Energy
Solar panels and wind turbines don't **pollute the environment.**

**1 Look and circle the correct option.**

1 

conserve water / pollute the environment

2 

use fossil fuels / plant trees

3 

recycle / send garbage to landfills

4 

save electricity / use clean energy

**2 Complete the phrases and answer. Which actions help the environment?**

1. ____________ trees
2. ____________ electricity
3. ____________ the environment
4. ____________ your carbon footprint
5. conserve ____________
6. send garbage to ____________
7. use clean ____________
8. use fossil ____________

**Recycle**
Where does your garbage go? Every day, cities **send** tons of **garbage to landfills.** But many materials shouldn't go there—they can be used again. Recycle paper, plastic, **glass** and metal.

**3 Match the verbs with the definitions.**

| | |
|---|---|
| 1. conserve | to protect a natural resource |
| 2. save | to introduce garbage and chemicals to a place |
| 3. recycle | to put something in the ground to grow |
| 4. pollute | to use less of something |
| 5. plant | to transform objects into new things |

**4** 12 **Listen and number the suggestions.**

☐ Eat less meat.

☐ Wear a sweater.

☐ Buy a new car.

☐ Read a book.

3 min **5 Think Fast!** Read and mark (✓) about you. Then calculate your score.

## How much do you care about the environment?

| | Always (+5) | Sometimes (+3) | Never (0) |
|---|---|---|---|
| 1. I use public transportation. | | | |
| 2. I use only the water that I need. | | | |
| 3. I recycle plastic, glass, metal and paper. | | | |
| 4. I save energy by turning off lights. | | | |
| 5. My family uses modern lightbulbs. | | | |
| 6. We sort our trash at home. | | | |

Scores: 24–30 points → Awesome! / 15–23 points → Not bad! / 0–15 → Try a little harder!

**Guess What!**
Fossil fuels like oil and gas come from plants that were alive millions of years ago!

**Glossary**

**carpool:** to arrange to travel together in the same car

**power plants:** factories that generate electricity

**soil:** earth; dirt

**glass:** a hard transparent material

## Grammar

**1** **Look at the picture and mark (✓) the actions that help the environment and (✗) actions that pollute the environment.**

**2** **Read the *Ask Miss Eco* column and underline the four environmental problems.**

44

# Ask Miss Eco

**Hi. My mom says I should pick up after my dog. I don't understand what harm it does. If I don't clean it, what will happen? (Danny 14)**
Your mom's right, Danny. Dog poop not only smells, it contains parasites and can cause infections in humans and animals. It also pollutes water. If more people pick up after their dogs, the city will be much cleaner. As a dog owner, it's your responsibility!

**Someone told me that noise pollution can cause physical damage. What will happen if I listen to loud music? (Carol, 15)**
If you listen to loud music, especially with headphones on, you will have permanent hearing problems by the age of 40. There is already a lot of noise around you—planes, cars, motorcycles, radios and heavy machinery—these all cause noise pollution.

**I heard the term "light pollution." Does this kind of pollution really exist? (Theo, 13)**
That's an interesting question, Theo. Light pollution does exist. There are more and more lights everywhere. Artificial lights in towns and cities stop us from having a clear view of the sky. If we use lights everywhere, we will soon forget what a starry sky is!

**If I take a shower every day, will I use less water than if I take a bath? (Olivia, 14)**
That is correct, Olivia. You use 26 liters of water for a quick shower and about 94 liters of water for a bath. You will always use less water if you take showers than if you take a bath. But don't stay in the shower for more than 10 minutes!

**What are the main causes of air pollution and what can I do? (Sean, 16)**
Where do I start? Air pollution is caused mainly by emissions from factories and from burning fossil fuels like coal and gasoline. Cars produce a lot of bad gases, which causes air pollution. The next time your father or mother takes you to school, make sure you take a friend or two. If we share our cars, there will be fewer cars in the streets and less pollution in the air!

## First Conditional

We use First Conditional to talk about future possibilities:
**If we keep** using cars, air pollution **will get** worse.
There **will be** shortages **if we continue** to waste water.

**3 Read the magazine article again and complete the sentences.**

1. If more people pick up after their dogs, ______________________.
2. What will happen ______________________?
3. ______________________, we will soon forget what a starry sky is!
4. ______________________, will I use less water than if I take a bath?
5. If we share our cars, ______________________.



**4 [13] Listen to the interview and mark (✓) the topics that the people talk about.**

| | | | | | |
|---|---|---|---|---|---|
| washing the dishes | ☐ | plastic waste | ☐ | consuming energy | ☐ |
| washing clothes | ☐ | recycling waste | ☐ | using electricity at home | ☐ |

**5 [13] Listen again and mark *T* (True) or *F* (False).**

1. If we use compact fluorescent bulbs instead of regular lightbulbs, we will save 25% more energy. T F
2. Washing dishes by hand uses less water than a dishwasher. T F
3. Using cold water in a washing machine is not as good for washing clothes as using hot water. T F
4. The biggest user of energy at home is electrical equipment. T F
5. Every time we leave the refrigerator door open, we waste energy. T F

5 min

**6 Think Fast! Read the conditions and consequences. Then connect the sentences using the first conditional.**

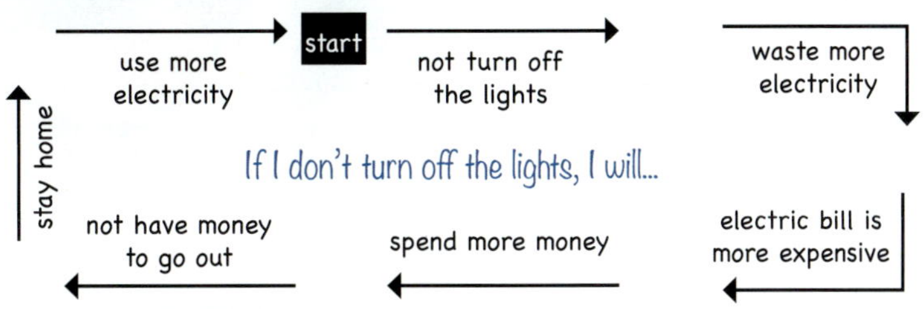


**Guess What!**
In the United States, it takes 25 large power stations to provide electricity for all the refrigerators in the country for one year.

# Reading and Writing

**1 Look and write the headings.**

Being Vegetarian
Wearing Fur Coats
Keeping Animals in Zoos

I'm not against wearing animal fur. We use **leather** for shoes, belts and jackets—so why shouldn't we use fur for coats and hats? ☐

I don't agree with killing animals for their fur. It's wrong and it's **cruel**. There are many alternatives that are **stylish** and warm. ☐

Zoos are good for the environment. They help to conserve animals that are in danger in the wild. And they're a great way for kids to learn about wild animals. ☐

I'm against having zoos. Animals are **confined** in small areas so they can't move freely. Besides, they are fed by humans, so they can't hunt for food. They will never be able to live in the wild again. ☐

There are many reasons to be vegetarian. Firstly, meat isn't good for our bodies. Secondly, it isn't right to kill animals for food. And finally, it requires a lot of water and land to keep animals. Growing **crops** is much less **wasteful**. ☐

There's nothing wrong with eating meat. Humans are omnivores, and meat does have a lot of protein. Plus, it tastes really good! ☐

**2 Read the statements. Write *F* (For) or *A* (Against).**

**3** **Read the statements on page 46 again. Which arguments do you agree with? Underline the arguments that sound more convincing.**

**4** **Complete the opinion expressions.**

1. There are ______________________________ to be vegetarian.
2. There's ______________________________ with eating meat.
3. Zoos are ______________________________ the environment.
4. I'm ______________________________ having zoos.
5. I'm ______________________________ wearing animal fur.
6. I ______________________________ with killing animals for their fur.

**5** **Choose a topic from page 46. Write a sentence to state your opinion using an expression from Activity 4.**

______________________________________________

**6** **Add two or three reasons to support your opinion.**

______________________________________________

______________________________________________

______________________________________________

**Be Strategic!**
Be more persuasive. State your opinion in a clear way and give reasons to support your opinion.

**Stop and Think!** How can you develop an informed opinion about something?

## Glossary

**leather:** a material made from animal skin

**cruel:** causing pain and suffering

**stylish:** in style; fashionable

**confined:** locked in an area

**crops:** plants that are used for food

**wasteful:** using resources in an inefficient way

# Culture

**1 Read and number the photos.**

1. In Japan, many businesses have *Maneki neko* cat figures for good luck!
2. The people of Okinawa, in southern Japan, have very distinct food. One dish is *umi budo*—a type of **seaweed** that tastes like **caviar**.
3. Sumo wrestling is a popular sport in Japan. Good sumo wrestlers should be very heavy. They **skip** breakfast and sleep after meals to help them gain weight!
4. In the spring, white and pink cherry **blossoms** appear all over Japan. People have picnics and parties in parks to enjoy them. There are even cherry-blossom flavored snacks.

**2** **Read the article. Is nuclear energy a good option? Why or why not?**

# Nuclear Energy in Japan

Japan is home to 127 million people, and is about the size of the State of California. Japan doesn't have a lot of fossil fuels, so it needs to buy them from other countries to generate electricity. They also have more than 50 nuclear reactors, which can generate energy without carbon emissions. But now they're only using a few of these reactors. What happened?

In 2011, there was a large earthquake near the coast of Japan. It was very powerful, measuring 9.0 on the Richter scale. It caused a tsunami that damaged some nuclear reactors at the Fukushima power plant. The damaged reactors emit *radiation*, energy particles that can make people very sick. Everyone who lived near the power plant was **evacuated**—nearly 450,000 people—and even after several years, more than 100,000 people can't return to their homes. In addition, the power plant continues to **leak radioactive** water, which is collected so that it doesn't flow into the ocean. It leaks several tons of contaminated water every day. Now a plan is in place to reduce the flow of water, but it will take 30 to 40 years to clean up the site.

For this reason, people in Japan don't see nuclear energy as a safe option. They plan to close the last few nuclear power plants. Now they have an opportunity to use and develop new forms of clean energy.



**3** 14 **Listen and answer. Why is the town of Kamikatsu a special place?**

**4** 14 **Listen again and circle *T* (True) or *F* (False).**

1. Kamikatsu is a small town in northern Japan. T F
2. The population of Kamikatsu is about 2,000. T F
3. They don't have a garbage truck. T F
4. They wash their garbage. T F
5. There are 20 recycling categories. T F
6. They make new things using old clothes. T F

**Stop and Think!** How can you create less garbage?

## Glossary

**seaweed:** an ocean plant

**caviar:** fish eggs

**skip:** to not do something

**blossoms:** flowers

**evacuated:** moved to a safe place

**leak:** to lose liquid from a container

**radioactive:** contaminated with radiation

# Project

**1** **Look and match the symbols with the slogans.**

 ☐

 ☐

 ☐

 ☐

 ☐

**2** 15 **Listen to the scripts and mark (✓) the topics.**

**3** 15 **Number the missing fragments of each script. Then listen again and check.**

1. Be cool. Don't **litter**. 2. garbage trucks don't collect 3. in bottles, bags
4. reduce, reuse and recycle 5. throw **trash** out of their cars 6. will have less trash
7. will ever visit our area 8. sort our trash

| | |
|---|---|
| **Script 1** | In general, people in our community care about the environment. We ___ and take paper, plastic, glass and metal to the special **dumpster** to recycle. The problem is that the dumpster is always full because the ___ recycling every day. I really think they should, so that people don't have to leave the trash around the dumpster. It is also important to reduce the number of containers we use. If we reuse containers, we ___. So remember: ___! |
| **Script 2** | A growing problem in our neighborhood is littering. Some people ___ or leave it in the park, on the grass. In some places, the ground is covered ___ and **wrappers**. It's **infuriating**! If people continue littering like this, no one ___, we will harm the wildlife and pollute the environment. We should work together, clean up the mess and live in a healthy and beautiful place. It is time to say: ___! |

**Guess What!**
You don't need to be an important political figure to change your community. There are thousands—maybe millions—of teen activists in the world. They see a problem and look for a way to solve it.

**Glossary**

**litter:** throw garbage in public places
**trash:** garbage
**dumpster:** a large container for trash
**wrappers:** covers for food items
**infuriating:** making someone very angry

**4 Make a mini documentary about your community.**

1. Work with a group. Discuss different activities that help or hurt the environment in your community.
2. Choose one or more activities to feature in your mini documentary.
3. Write a script similar to the one in Activity 3 for your video. Explain why an action has a positive or negative impact.
4. Make a three minute video to present your information. Use images from the community to demonstrate the activities.

# Review

## 1 Read and complete the sentences.

conserve  emissions  energy  fossil  landfills  planting  pollute  saves

1. Many cars and buses use ____________________ fuels.
2. Turn off the lights when you leave a room. It ____________________ electricity.
3. Reuse and recycle. Send less garbage to ____________________.
4. ____________________ water! It's a precious resource.
5. You can improve your neighborhood by ____________________ trees.
6. Traditional power plants ____________________ the environment.
7. Use clean ____________________ like solar and wind energy.
8. Buying local products is a good way to reduce your carbon ____________________.

52

## 2 Look and label the actions.

1  c____________________ w____________________

2  s____________________ e____________________

3  p____________________ the e____________________

4  r____________________ c____________________ e____________________

5  s____________________ g____________________ to l____________________

6  p____________________ t____________________

7  u____________________ c____________________ e____________________

8  u____________________ f____________________ f____________________

# Is it too late to save the planet?

**3 Read and circle the correct option.**

The climate is changing. The arctic is warming. Some cities have air pollution that makes people sick. Is it too late to save the planet? I don't think so. If we (1) **make / will** make changes now, we (2) **make / can make** a difference. With new technologies, we can reduce our carbon footprint to zero. It's easy to think only countries and companies can change things, but small decisions are important, too. We (3) **have / will have** a lot less garbage if we (4) **start / will start** reusing and recycling more. And if we (5) **choose / will choose** earth-friendly products—without toxic chemicals or a large carbon footprint—companies (6) **make / will make** more earth-friendly products. If everyone (7) **cares / will care** about the environment, the situation (8) **improve / will improve.** Make a change today!



**4 Unscramble the questions.**

1. what / on / the / will / we / throw / happen / if / trash / ground / ?

   ______________________________

   The city will look dirty.
2. happen / what / if / the / we / pollute / will / air / ?

   ______________________________

   People will get sick.
3. pollute / what / happen / we / the / will / if / oceans / ?

   ______________________________

   Fish and animals will die.
4. recycle / will / happen / what / we / if / ?

   ______________________________

   We'll send less garbage to landfills.
5. we / clean / happen / will / what / use / energy / if / ?

   ______________________________

   We'll have clean air and water.

# Just for Fun

**1 Read and complete the sentences.**

it will produce oxygen and clean the air
you will keep them out of landfills
you won't need any electricity or use any fossil fuels
you can reduce your carbon footprint by 500%
you will save up to 500 liters per month

**Conserve Water**

If you turn off the water when you wash your hair, ____________________!

**Stop Sending Garbage to Landfills**

Buy a cloth bag and use it when you shop. If you stop using plastic bags, ____________________—and prevent them from polluting the environment.

**Reduce Carbon Emissions**

If you eat chicken instead of beef, ____________________!

**Save Electricity**

You don't need to buy solar panels to use clean energy. If you use natural sunlight instead of a lamp, ____________________!

**Plant Something... Anything!**

Planting trees helps the environment, but all plants do! If you keep a small plant in your house, ____________________.

**2 Look and classify the recyclable materials (1=plastic, 2=paper, 3=glass).**

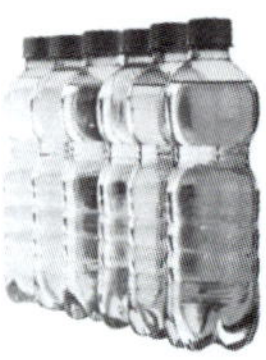

water bottles ☐

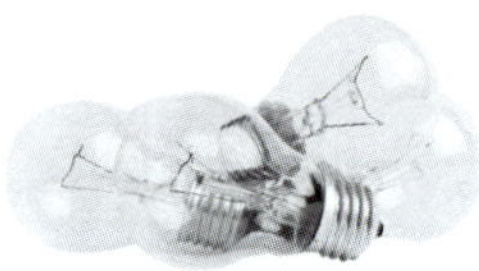

lightbulbs ☐

newspapers ☐

jars ☐

shampoo bottles ☐

cardboard boxes ☐

soda bottles ☐

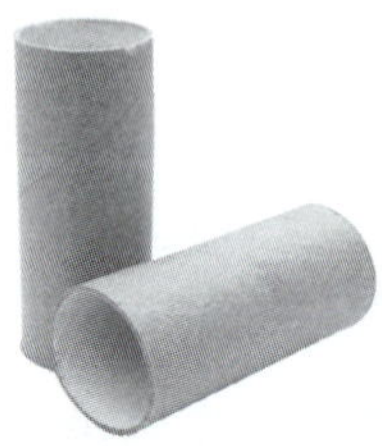

toilet paper rolls ☐

# 4

# What's your passion?

# Vocabulary

**1 Look and underline the topic.**

a. school activities     b. being a fan     c. house chores

**2 [16] Listen and number the expressions.**

be good at

stand in line

wear a hat

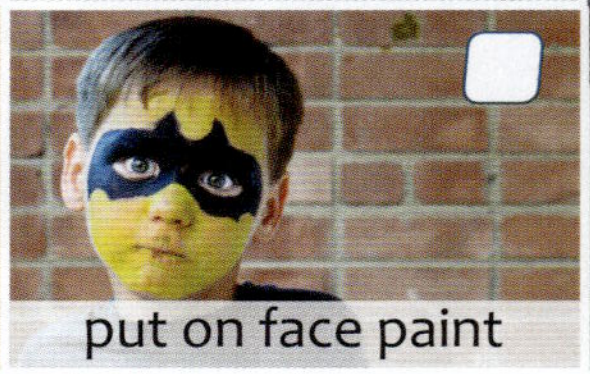
put on face paint

be a fan of

put up posters

collect action figures

dress up as characters

get an autograph

wear team colors

**3 [16] Read and complete the speech bubbles. Then listen again and check.**

collect   colors   face   fan   get   good   hat   in   up (2x)

MY PASSION IS FOOTBALL! I CAN'T WAIT FOR THE FALL WHEN FOOTBALL SEASON STARTS! IT'S FUN TO WEAR TEAM ________________ ON GAME DAY. THEY'RE GREEN AND YELLOW. I PUT ON ________________ PAINT, TOO. IT'S MESSY, BUT LOTS OF FUN. AND I WEAR A SILLY ________________ FOR GOOD LUCK.

I AM A HUGE ________________ OF ZOMBIES. I PUT ________________ ZOMBIE POSTERS ALL OVER MY ROOM. MY FRIENDS AND I DRESS ________________ AS MOVIE CHARACTERS. I'M REALLY ________________ AT MOVIE MAKEUP, WITH **FAKE BLOOD** AND EVERYTHING.

## 4 Read and match.

| | |
|---|---|
| 1. stand in | colors |
| 2. be good | at |
| 3. get an | as characters |
| 4. dress up | fan of |
| 5. be a | hat |
| 6. wear team | autograph |
| 7. collect | line |
| 8. put on | face paint |
| 9. wear a | posters |
| 10. put up | action figures |

## 5 Read and complete the sentences.

1. Our ______________ are blue and orange.
2. I'll ______________ all day to get a concert ticket.
3. You're really ______________ playing the saxophone.
4. I ______________ soccer **jerseys**. I have eight of them!
5. My brothers always go to conventions to get ______________.
6. My friends and I ______________ face paint to every game.
7. We need to ______________ as dragons for the party.
8. Are you a ______________ of superhero movies?

## 6 Describe the picture using the expressions from Activity 4.

______________________________

______________________________

______________________________

______________________________

______________________________

______________________________

## 7 Think Fast! Write the fan activities in alphabetical order. Which activities do you do?

3 min

**Guess What!**

Did you ever miss a character at the end of a book or movie? *Fanfiction* is a writing genre where people write stories about characters. They often imagine new adventures or invent alternate endings.

**Glossary**

**fake:** not real

**blood:** red fluid in the body

**geek:** a fan of something unusual

**signature:** a person's name in cursive

**jersey:** a shirt used in team sports as part of a uniform

# Grammar

**1** 🎧[17] **Read the flyer. Then listen and write *C* (Carrie) or *A* (Andrea).**

1. She's going to dress up as Katniss Everdeen. ______
2. She's going to dress up as Effie Trinket. ______

58

**2** 🎧[17] **Listen again and complete the phrases using intensifiers. What is the role of intensifiers?**

1. really ____________________
2. a bit ____________________
3. pretty ____________________
4. extremely ____________________
5. so ____________________

| Intensifiers | |
|---|---|
| extremely | → !!!! |
| so | → !!! |
| really | → !!! |
| pretty | → !! |
| a bit | → ! |

**3** **Read and complete the dialogue.**

Will: Hey, Lauren.

Lauren: Hi, Will.

Will: Did you see the new Star Trek movie?

Lauren: Yeah. It was (1) ____________________ (!!) cool. The special effects were (2) ____________________ (!!!) amazing.

Brian: Hi, Will! Hi, Lauren!

Lauren: Hi, Brian! What did you think about the Star Trek movie?

Brian: It was spectacular!—I mean (3) ____________________ (!!!!) entertaining. I'm seeing it again tomorrow night.

Will: Can I come along?

Brian: Sure! Coliseum Cinema?

Will: That's (4) ____________________ (!) far for me. Can we go somewhere closer?

Brian: No problem. Are you coming, too, Lauren?

Lauren: Sorry, guys. I have a big soccer match. But have fun!

**4** Listen and mark (✓) the correct option. [18]

## Already, Yet

We use *yet* in questions and negative sentences:
Did you play any games **yet**?
I didn't play any games **yet**.

We use *already* for affirmative sentences:
I **already** played three games.

1. Jo is dressed up as ______ ☐ a dragon. ☐ an **alien.**
2. Elsie ______ wearing a costume. ☐ is ☐ isn't
3. Elsie ______ for the **contest** yet. ☐ signed up ☐ didn't sign up
4. Jo ______ signed up for the contest. ☐ already ☐ yet

**5** Look at the map and write the sentences using *already* or *yet*.

1. Jo and Elsie / play / some games

______________________________

2. they / not have / any snacks

______________________________

3. they / not watch / a movie

______________________________

4. they / see / the fan art exhibition

______________________________

5. they / go / to the costume contest

______________________________

### Glossary

**alien:** an extraterrestrial life form
**contest:** a competition

3 min **6 Think Fast!** Imagine you are at the Sci-Fi Festival. Ask and answer five questions about the event.

# Reading & Speaking

**1 Read the descriptions. Which text describes a good listener?**

1. It's not always cool to be friends with your mom, but my mom is the best. When I want to talk to her, she stops what she's doing and pays attention to me. She asks me things. I'm glad we're **close**.

2. My friend and I hang out a lot, but she's always looking at her phone. I'm never sure that she cares about what I'm saying. We have fun, though.

3. My brother and I never get along. The minute I say anything, he **interrupts** me. Or if I need to ask him something, he doesn't pay attention. He always asks, "Huh?" or "What?" instead of listening the first time!

Text ________ describes a good listener.

### Be Strategic!

Active listening is an important communication—and speaking—skill. To be an active listener, concentrate on the other person's message. Be prepared to ask questions to check your understanding and to show interest.

60

**2 Read the conversation and underline the questions.**

**Lily:** My name is Lily and this is my new friend Renée. We're practicing active listening for our English class. What's your favorite activity, Renée? What are you passionate about?

**Renée:** That's pretty easy—cheerleading. I've **been** a cheerleader since I was five years old.

**Lily:** What do you do, I mean, as a cheerleader?

**Renée:** Well, we do cheers—like **chants**—and gymnastics at football and basketball games. And we go to cheerleading competitions, too.

**Lily:** What's that like?

**Renée:** It's a lot like a gymnastics or dance competition. We learn a routine and perform it in front of **judges**. We use pop songs for our routines. It's a lot of fun.

**Lily:** Is cheerleading a sport? I never thought of it that way before.

**Renée:** It is! And cheerleaders are athletes. We lift weights and exercise a lot.

**Lily:** How often do you **work out**?

**Renée:** I go to the gym almost every day.

**Lily:** I'm really impressed. When is your next competition? Maybe I can come and **cheer you on**!

**Renée:** It's this Saturday! Sure! Come and see us!

### Glossary

**close:** with a good relationship

**interrupt:** to speak when someone else is speaking

**been:** the past participle of the verb *be*

**chants:** phrases repeated with a rhythm

**judges:** officials who give a score to a performer

**work out:** to exercise

**cheer you on:** to encourage someone to do something

**3 Complete and match.**

1. What __________ you do?
2. What's that __________?
3. __________ cheerleading a sport?
4. How __________ do you work out?
5. __________ is your next competition?

It's this Saturday.

It is!

It's a lot like gymnastics...

We do cheers...

I go to the gym almost every day.

**4 🎧19 Read the dialogue and complete the questions. Then listen and check.**

do how what when where

**Patrick:** So __________ is your passion, Damian?

**Damian:** My passion is train spotting. I'm a total train geek. I love trains, and I learn everything about very specific **engines**. Then I go places to take pictures of them.

**Patrick:** I don't know very much about train spotting. Aren't all trains the same? __________ are they different?

**Damian:** Each engine is kind of unique. It has different colors and logos, according to the company it belongs to. And they have different numbers on them. They even have different **horns**.

**Patrick:** __________ did you get interested in trains?

**Damian:** When I was little.

**Patrick:** And __________ do you go to see the trains?

**Damian:** I go to many places, but my favorite place is by the river. It's a really great place for pictures.

**Patrick:** __________ you have a favorite picture?

**Damian:** Yes. It's this one. A Union Pacific engine.

**Patrick:** That's pretty cool. Hey, thanks for sharing about your hobby.

**Damian:** You're welcome.

5 min

**5 Think Fast! Choose a dialogue to read aloud with a classmate. Can you do it without making any mistakes?**

**6 What are you passionate about? Ask and answer with a classmate.**

**Stop and Think!** What activities do you dislike? Is it ever good to do activities that are boring or unpleasant?

**Glossary**

**engine:** the part of a train with a motor, usually at the front of the train

**horns:** a part of a vehicle that makes a loud noise as a warning

# Culture

**1** Look at the map. Do you know what country it is?

**2** Read and number.

1. Pakistan is a country in South Asia. It borders four different countries: India, Afghanistan, Iran and China. In Pakistan, the main languages are English, Urdu, and Punjabi.
2. The largest city in Pakistan is Karachi, but the capital is Islamabad. *Abad* means city in Urdu.
3. K-2, the world's second highest peak, is located in Pakistan.
4. *Roh* is a popular drink in Pakistan. It's made of sugarcane juice and spices.
5. Cricket is the most popular sport in Pakistan, but field hockey is the national sport. Baseball is pretty popular there, too.
6. The Thar desert is located on the border between Pakistan and India. It's the world's ninth largest sub-tropical desert.
7. Pakistan makes more than 50% of the world's soccer balls and is a big producer of cotton.
8. Malala Yousafzai is a Pakistani activist. She believes strongly in education, especially for girls. In 2014, at the age of 17, she received the Nobel Peace Prize.

**3** 🎧20 Listen and complete the table.

| | Cricket | Street Cricket |
|---|---|---|
| History | the 18th century | the 19________s |
| Teams | ________ players | ________ players |
| Equipment | a bat, a leather ball, helmets, pads and gloves | a ________ ball and a ________ |
| Played | on a cricket pitch | in the ________ |

## 4 Read the article and write the headlines.

Sports
Agriculture in Pakistan
Other Attractions
An Annual Event

___________________________

Agriculture is a major industry in Pakistan. Seventy percent of the population works in this industry. The most important crops are **wheat**, sugarcane, cotton and rice. Pakistan is also the world's largest producer of mangoes. Livestock like cows, sheep, buffalo and goats are also important.

___________________________

In March of 2015, the Pakistani city of Lahore hosted the National Horse and Cattle Show. It took place in Fortress Stadium and lasted for several days. The show is a local tradition with a long history. It features exciting sports and entertaining shows.

___________________________

The Horse and Cattle Show is famous for equestrian sports: horse racing, polo and a local sport called *tent pegging*. Tent pegging is an ancient sport where the participant must hit a small **target** with a sword or a **lance**.

___________________________

There are many things to see at the National Horse and Cattle Show. People do **stunts** on motorcycles. There are **skydivers**. You can watch a military parade or dog races. There are dog shows and cattle shows, where participants compete to have the best animal. There are even events with dancing horses and camels. At night, there are fireworks and performances with **torches**.

## 5 Find and write the word.

1. the nationality of a person, place or thing in Pakistan ___________
2. three cities in Pakistan ___________
3. the national sport ___________
4. a famous activist from Pakistan ___________
5. an important industry ___________
6. a common fruit in Pakistan ___________
7. the season of the horse and cattle show ___________
8. in tent pegging, a person rides this animal ___________

**Stop and Think!** How are farmers important to a community?

### Glossary

**wheat:** a plant seed used to make bread

**target:** the object of attention or attack

**lance:** a long, sharp pole

**stunts:** tricks

**skydivers:** people who jump from a plane with parachutes

**torches:** sticks to carry fire from one place to another

## ARE YOU A SPORTS FAN?

- Come and see the New England Patriots at Gillette Stadium! Their team colors are red, white, silver and blue.

- Visit historic Fenway Park and see the Red Sox play! It's a Boston pastime!

- Are you into basketball? Don't miss the Boston Celtics at TD Garden!

- The Boston Bruins are six-time Stanley Cup champions!

**1 Look at the Fan Activities brochure. Who is this brochure for?**

- sports fans ☐
- music fans ☐
- international food fans ☐
- history fans ☐
- science fans ☐
- art and literature fans ☐

**2 Read the brochure and circle the correct option.**

1. These are activities you can do in **Atlanta** / **Boston** / **Chicago**.
2. The Red Sox are a **basketball** / **baseball** / **hockey** team.
3. The Stanley Cup is a **football** / **basketball** / **hockey** trophy.
4. Visits to the **science museum** / **aquarium** / **observatory** are free in the evenings.
5. *Doro wot* is an **Irish** / **Ethiopian** / **Italian** dish.

## ARE YOU A SCIENCE FAN?

The Museum of Science is an excellent destination! Learn about dinosaurs, butterflies, clean energy and space travel.

Come to see the New England Aquarium! They have penguins, sea turtles and marine animals. You can even go on a whale watch!

Are you an astronomy fan? Boston has seven different observatories. Night time admission is free!

## ARE YOU A FAN OF INTERNATIONAL CUISINE?

Irish heritage is important in Boston, and there are dozens of Irish restaurants to try. Shepherd's pie is a classic dish!

Ethiopian food is also popular in Boston. Doro wot (chicken in sauce) is a popular dish, but be careful! It can be very spicy!

Every American city has Mexican restaurants, but Boston has restaurants from many Latin American countries! Try Chilean or Peruvian food today!

Tacos

Polish Pierogi

Boston offers European cuisines, too: enjoy dishes from Spain, Italy, Poland, Germany or Greece! Mmm!

**3** **Choose a city or region and complete the mind map. What kinds of fans are happy there? What activities can they do?**

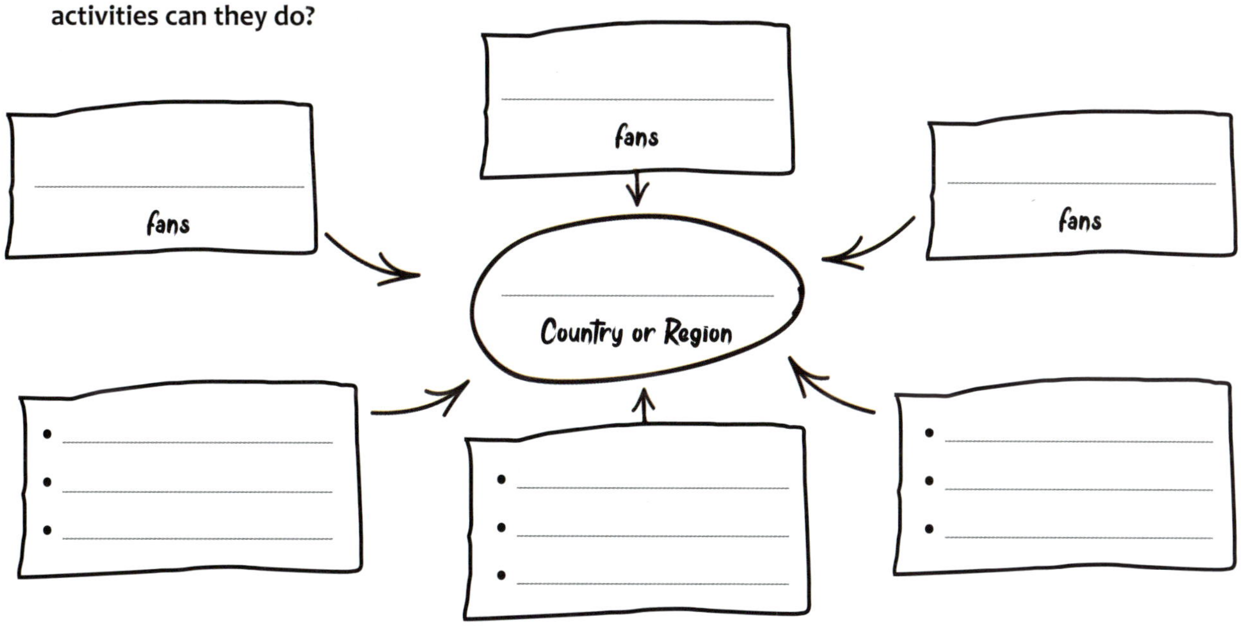


**4** **Make a Fan Activities brochure and present it to the class.**

# Review

**1 Complete the questions. Then read and match.**

1. Do you collect ____________ figures?
2. What are you ____________ at?
3. Did you ever ____________ an autograph from someone?
4. How long would you ____________ in line for something?
5. What are you a ____________ of?
6. Do you ever ____________ up as a character?

I'm a fan of cooking competitions. I love watching them!

Yes! I collect DC Comics figures. Mostly the Green Lantern.

Maybe for half an hour. I'm not a very patient person.

Only on Halloween! Last year, I went as Kylo Ren from Star Wars.

When I was little, a famous basketball player signed my T-shirt.

I'm good at drawing. I do a lot of manga.

**2 Look and write a fan activity.**

1  ____________

3  ____________

2  ____________

4  ____________

**3 Read and underline the intensifiers. Write them on the lines.**

I have many interests, but I'm a big fan of *Doctor Who*. It's an extremely popular sci-fi TV show from the UK. It's about a guy who has special powers—the Doctor. He can travel through time and space in a TARDIS. It looks like a blue police box, but it's really big inside. He fights against the Daleks. They're part alien, part robot, and they want to "exterminate" everyone. It's a lot of fun to watch *Doctor Who*. When I first saw the show, I thought it was a bit silly, but now I think it's so awesome. Even my friends think it's pretty cool.

1. ____________ ☐ 3. ____________ ☐
2. ____________ ☐ 4. ____________ ☐ 5. ____________ ☐

**4 Look and write *!*, *!!*, *!!!* or *!!!!* next to the intensifiers.**

**5 Read and describe using intensifiers. Choose and circle the adjective.**

1. your town or city — It's ____________ big / small.
2. your favorite movie — It's ____________ exciting / romantic.
3. kids' movies — They're ____________ fun / silly.
4. typical American food — It's ____________ good / bad.

**6 Write sentences using the cues and *already* or *yet*.**

1. we / see the fan art exhibition → +

____________________________________________

2. Sam / get the concert tickets → -

____________________________________________

3. Allison / watch the new movie → ?

____________________________________________

4. you / complete your costume → ?

____________________________________________

5. they / read the book → -

____________________________________________

# Just for Fun

**1 Read and mark (✓) the friends' interests.**

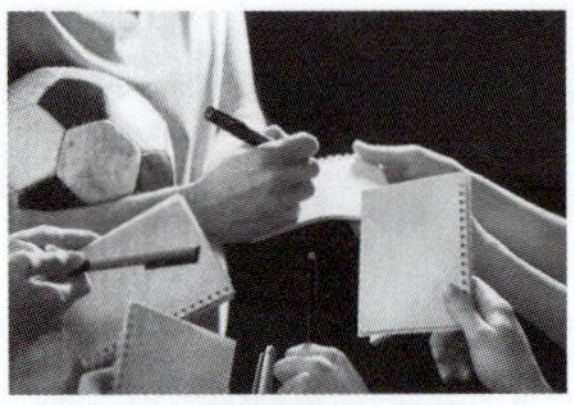

Kylie, Olivia, Will, Jake and Max have many interests, but they're all different. Can you guess who likes what?

Kylie isn't interested in sports. She doesn't go to games or have any favorite athletes. She does like to collect things, though. She's always buying new action figures.



Olivia likes sports a lot, and she goes to all of the games at her school. She supports her team at every game.

Will is also interested in sports. He goes to games all over the world, and has a big collection of autographed hats, balls and T-shirts.

Jake is a movie fan. He memorizes lines and facts about the actors. He has movie posters all over his room.

Max isn't a sports fan or a movie fan. He likes wearing costumes, and when he isn't dressed up, he's at home playing video games.

| | collects athletes' autographs | dresses up as video game characters | collects action figures | is a fan of a team | collects movie posters |
|---|---|---|---|---|---|
| Kylie | | | | | |
| Olivia | | | | | |
| Will | | | | | |
| Jake | | | | | |
| Max | | | | | |

5

# How much do you remember?

# Vocabulary

**1** Look and number the pictures.

☐ I made coffee for my mom, but I **made a mistake**. I added salt, not sugar!

☐ I **bought a lot of souvenirs** on my trip to London: a T-shirt, a hat and lots of postcards.

☐ I **took care of** my puppy, Zak. I fed him, gave him water, and took him for walks every day.

☐ We went to a big amusement park in Copenhagen. We **had a lot of fun**!

☐ My grandpa **forgot** my birthday. I was very sad that day.

☐ I **fell in love with** a girl in my class. We were six years old. Her name was Suzie.

☐ I **got in trouble** for breaking my phone. My parents were very angry at me.

☐ I was on vacation and my suitcase **got lost**. The airline put it on a different plane.

**2** **Read and circle the correct option.**

1. I **took care of / forgot** my baby brother while my mom was working.
2. I **made a mistake / had a lot of fun** and dialed a wrong number.
3. She **got in trouble / got lost** for arriving home late.
4. I **forgot / bought** a present for my friend and she loved it.
5. He **fell in love with / got lost** his dad's new car.

**3** 21 **Listen and match the people with the keepsakes.**

seashell

toy car

necklace

drawing

baby tooth

**Guess What!**

Photos and *keepsakes*—objects from important events—are common ways to remember the past. But music, smells and flavors can also help you remember information and experiences.

**4** **Read the description. Then write the name of the keepsake.**

1. It's shiny. It's metal with tiny white crystals. Maybe they're diamonds. ____________
2. It is red. One of the wheels is broken. ____________
3. It's smooth and shiny. It's pink on the inside and white and brown on the outside.
____________
4. It's small and white. It's not really shiny. ____________
5. It's in an old notebook. It's a dinosaur with big teeth. ____________

1 min **5** **Think Fast! Classify the keepsakes.**

| something that you make | something you wear | something you play with | something that falls out | something you find in nature |
| --- | --- | --- | --- | --- |
| | | | | |

# Grammar

**1 Look and number the scenes.**

**Past Continuous**

We use Past Continuous to describe actions that happen for a period of time in the past:
The children **were playing** all day.
My computer **wasn't working** yesterday.

**2** $^{22}$ **Listen and underline the cause of the problem.**

a. The weather was bad.

b. One of the swimmers got tired.

c. The currents were strong.

**3** $^{22}$ **Listen again and and circle *T* (True) or *F* (False).**

| | | |
|---|---|---|
| 1. A family was relaxing at the beach. | T | F |
| 2. A man and kids weren't having fun in the sea. | T | F |
| 3. Some tourists saw the family and **raised the alarm.** | T | F |
| 4. Some **lifeguards** were teaching a course nearby. | T | F |
| 5. A man was crying. | T | F |

1 min **4 Think Fast! Find and underline the verbs in the past continuous in Activity 3.**

**Glossary**

**exhausted:** very tired

**raise the alarm:** to call for help

**lifeguards:** expert swimmers trained to rescue swimmers at pools and beaches

**lucky:** fortunate

## Past Continuous and Past Simple: *When*

Past Continuous + *when* + Past Simple → a continuous action that is interrupted:

The family **was swimming** when strong currents **pulled** them away from the beach.

Past Continuous  Past Simple

## 5 Match the parts of the sentences.

1. Three members of a family were swimming (...)
2. Other family members were relaxing at the beach
3. Lifeguards were teaching a first-aid course
4. When we located the family,

- when they heard the dad shouting for help.
- the children were crying.
- when they got into trouble.
- when they realized there was a problem and raised the alarm.

## 6 Read the excerpts and write the headings.

An Earthquake  A Tornado  A Flood

______________________

It was a typical morning in Hudson, Ohio. (1) Most people were driving to work while others were shopping or going to school. (2) While the crew at the local fire station were cleaning the fire engines, Chief Brown was having his morning coffee. (3) He was checking his e-mail when he heard the phone. He answered and dropped his coffee on the floor. They had a real problem and it was coming in their direction at 100 kilometers per hour...

______________________

Sarah was on vacation in Acapulco with her parents and a dog. One day at the beach, (4) Sarah was playing with the dog while her parents were swimming in the sea. (5) She was just throwing a ball when she felt the earth moving under her feet. She turned around and saw the lifeguards shouting for people to evacuate the beaches. The palm trees started to move from side to side...

______________________

(6) David was looking out the window at the river while his mother was preparing breakfast. (7) He was thinking about the heavy rain when he saw that the water level in the river was going up quickly. (8) He was getting ready to tell his mom about it when someone knocked hard on their front door. He realized something was very wrong...

## Guess What!

When we talk about two simultaneous actions in the past, we use *while*:

I **was reading** a book while my dad **was watching** TV.

Past Continuous

Past Continuous

## 7 Read the underlined sentences in Activity 6. Then write *S* (Simultaneous) or *I* (Interrupted).

1. ____ 2. ____ 3. ____ 4. ____ 5. ____ 6. ____ 7. ____ 8. ____

# Reading & Listening

**1 Look and mark (✓) the topic of the article.**

☐ the parts of the brain and memory ☐ the organs of the body ☐ the brain

## How do you remember?

74

The brain is an organ that works like a very powerful computer. It doesn't have **wires** like a real computer, but it does have nerve cells, or *neurons*. Neurons transfer electricity and chemicals across the brain. One neuron can connect with many other neurons to create a *network*. When you learn something, new connections form between neurons. When you practice something—playing an instrument, doing ballet or using a foreign language—you make even more connections. More connections make it easier to do the activity again.

How do we make memories? A single memory can have many different types of information. Your brain processes the things you see, hear, smell, feel and think all at the same time. This information goes to a part of the brain called the *hippocampus*. The hippocampus is in the center of the brain, but it is connected to many other parts of the brain. After the hippocampus processes new memories, they go to the *cerebral cortex*. This is the "skin" of the brain. It isn't smooth like the outside of other organs. It has many folds, which helps it to **store** more information.

To remember information, the brain **replays** the pattern of electrical signals from the original event. This happens in many different parts of the brain so that you can remember what you saw, heard, smelled, felt and thought. Your brain is good at replaying memories in some situations. For example, you can easily remember the lyrics to your favorite song when it plays on the radio. The music you hear connects to similar information in your brain and helps you to remember the words. But if you try to remember the lyrics without the music, it's more difficult. For this reason, it can be difficult to remember facts for a test or a friend's phone number.

**2 Read the article and label.**

the cerebral cortex | the hippocampus | network | neuron

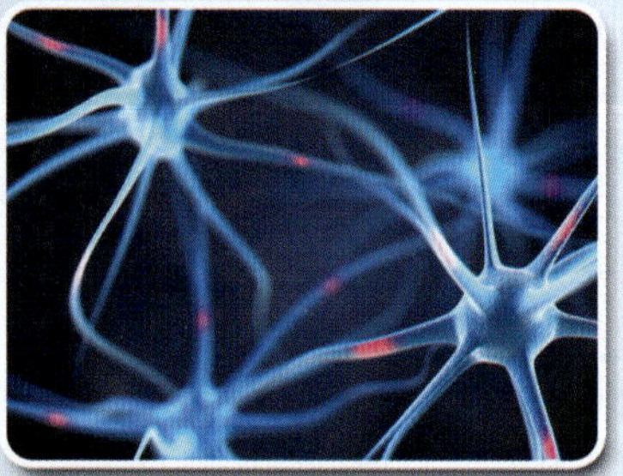

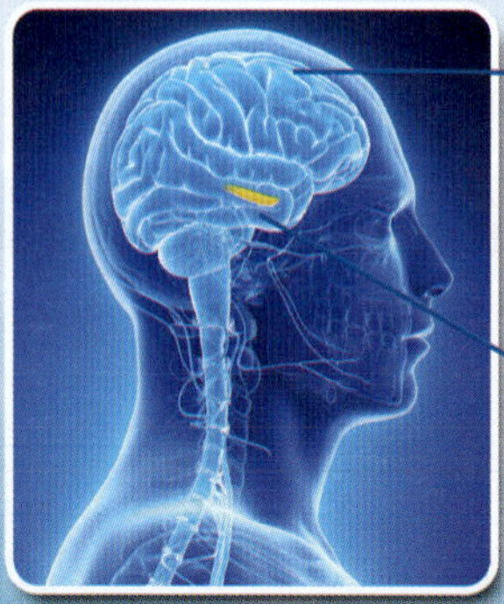

### Be Strategic!

You can get a general idea of a text by looking at photos and diagrams, but to understand more deeply, look for the connections between images and specific parts of the text.

### Glossary

**wires:** long, thin pieces of metal that conduct electricity

**store:** to keep; save

**replay:** to play something again

**3 Read again and complete the sentences.**

1. Nerve ____________ and neurons are the same things.
2. Neurons transfer ____________ and chemicals across the brain.
3. New ____________ form when you learn something.
4. You get better at an activity when your ____________ have more connections.
5. Memories form in the ____________ in the center of the brain.
6. Then memories go to the ____________ cortex.
7. When you remember something, your brain ____________ the pattern of electrical signals.

**4 23 Listen and circle the correct option.**

1. It's easy to let **technology / computers** remember for you.
   - ____________
   - ____________

2. Remembering keeps your brain active and **healthy / ready**.
   - ____________

3. The **first / next** strategy is to take care of yourself.
   - ____________
   - ____________
   - ____________

4. Write **things / notes** down.
   - ____________

5. **Give / Get** your brain a job.
   - ____________

**5 23 Read and complete the notes in Activity 4. Then listen again and check.**

manage stress | like a muscle | teach someone | information online | enough sleep | your phone | healthy diet | pen or pencil

**Guess What!**
Mnemonic devices are strategies to help you remember specific information. For example, making a chant or song can help you to remember lists or names.

3 min **6 Think Fast! Choose one item and try to memorize the information. Can you remember it when time is up?**

# Culture

**1 Read and complete the sentences.**

Ayers Rock 3% didgeridoo kangaroo forty-five thousand

1. Aboriginal Australians migrated to the country more than ____________ years ago.
2. Aboriginal peoples constitute ____________ of the Australian population.
3. ____________ or *Uluru* is a sacred mountain for the Aboriginal Australians.
4. Aboriginal Australians are famous for the music played on a ____________, a type of wooden instrument.
5. Many words for animals and places in Australia come from their languages, for example, ____________, kookaburra and koala.

**2 Read the article. Then write the underlined words under the correct images.**

# Aboriginal Australians

Aboriginal Australians have a **remarkable** and ancient culture. In fact, they have the oldest living cultural history in the world. They believe that humans, animals, plants and rocks date to a period called Dreamtime. This is when the spirits appeared and created humans, animals and the landscape as it is today. When they finished creating everything, the spirits changed into trees, stars, rocks, **watering holes** and humans. Aboriginals refer to the act of creation as *Dreaming*.

The myths related to Dreaming are called *songlines*. Songlines contain details about the landscape, so by singing them in the right sequence, it was possible for Aboriginals to navigate **vast** distances across the Australian outback and survive in difficult conditions.

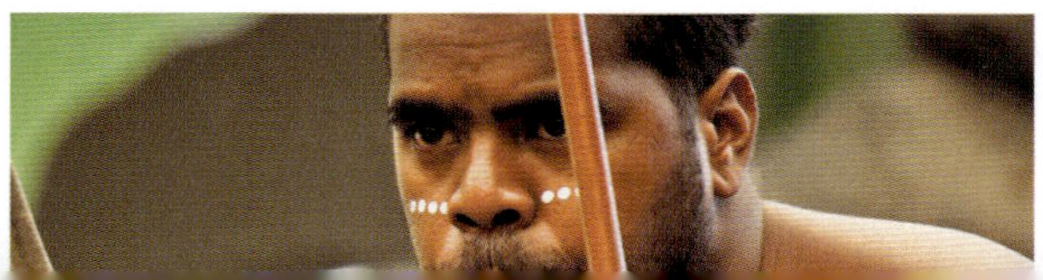

the objective of leaving traces of their culture for future generations. Art has always been important to the Aboriginal Australians as a link between past and present, myths and reality. You can find examples of rock paintings on the sacred mountain of Uluru in the central Australian desert.

For the last thirty years, the world has been hearing more and more about the Aboriginal arts. Today's artists still create traditional designs, such as **dot** painting to produce beautiful outline figures, animals and natural features of the landscape. In 2007, Emily Kame Kngwarreye's piece *Earth's Creation* sold for over a million dollars. ▪

Aboriginal art is also closely connected to the *Dreaming* myths. For thousands of years, Aboriginals were expressing their art on rock carvings, body painting and ground designs with

## 3 Look at the pictures. Do you know what place it is?

a r G t e ______ r e B r a r i ______ e R f e ______

## 4 [24] Listen and unscramble the name of the place.

## 5 [24] Listen again and number the questions in order.

- ☐ Are there any threats to the GBR?
- ☐ Is it a Natural Wonder of the World?
- ☐ Where is the GBR located?
- ☐ Is it true that you can see it from outer space?
- ☐ How big is it?
- ☐ How many types of fish live there?
- ☐ What is it made of?

## 6 Match the questions with the answers.

1. Yes, it is. ______
2. It's off the coast of Australia. ______
3. 1,500 types. ______
4. It is 2,000 km long and 180 m high. ______
5. It's made of coral. ______
6. Yes! ______
7. The GBR faces several threats. ______

**Stop and Think!** Are there natural wonders under threat in your country?

### Glossary

**remarkable:** extraordinary, special

**watering hole:** a place where you can find water

**vast:** very large

**dot:** a point

# Project

**1 Look at the timeline on page 79 and choose the correct option.**

1. What became available on October 23, 2001?
   a. iPod b. iPhone c. iPad
2. Facebook was online _____ Youtube.
   a. before b. after c. at the same time as
3. The 2012 Olympic Games opened in London on _____.
   a. June 18th b. July 4th c. July 27th
4. Aaron has _____ brothers and sisters.
   a. no b. two c. three
5. His birthday is in _____.
   a. June b. April c. December

**2 Classify the events from Aaron's timeline. Write *PE* or *WE* .**

Barack Obama _____
move to Dallas _____
Emily _____
*Harry Potter* _____
Facebook _____
Aaron's birth _____
iPod _____
kindergarten _____
baby Noah _____
Olympic Games _____
seventh grade _____
vacation in Spain _____
tsunami _____
YouTube _____

**3 List seven important personal events for you and your family. Write the dates.**

| Event | Date |
| --- | --- |
| _____ | _____ |
| _____ | _____ |
| _____ | _____ |
| _____ | _____ |
| _____ | _____ |
| _____ | _____ |
| _____ | _____ |

**4** **Make a personalized timeline. Use Aaron's timeline as a model.**

## My Personalized Timeline

by Aaron Taylor

**June 5, 2001** – I was born.

**October 23, 2001** – Stores began selling first generation iPod.

**November 4, 2001** – *Harry Potter and the Sorcerer's Stone* opened in movie theaters.

**April 23, 2003** – My sister Emily was born.

**February 4, 2004** – Mark Zuckerberg launched Facebook.

**December 26, 2004** – The deadliest tsunami in history occured in the Indian Ocean.

**February 14, 2005** – YouTube went online.

**August 28, 2006** – I started kindergarten.

**June 29, 2007** – The first iPhones went on the market.

**December 1, 2008** – My brother Noah was born.

**January 20, 2009** – Barack Obama became the first African American President of the United States.

**January 27, 2010** – The first iPads became available.

**May 2, 2011** – My family moved to Dallas, Texas.

**July 7, 2011** – *Harry Potter and the Deathly Hollows, Part 2* opened in the UK.

**July 27, 2012** – The 2012 Olympic Games opened in London.

**September 3, 2013** – I started seventh grade in junior high school.

**June 10, 2016** – I went on a trip to Barcelona, Spain.

# Review

**1 Unscramble names of keepsakes. Then read and number the questions.**

1. kalecnec ____________________
2. ybtb ohota ____________________
3. yat roc ____________________
4. ingradw ____________________
5. hessaell ____________________

☐ What can you wear on your neck?
☐ What do you find at the beach?
☐ What falls out as a child grows older?
☐ What is a form of art?
☐ What can you play with?

**2 Circle and correct the mistakes.**

1. I take care in my little brother. ____________
2. She buys much souvenirs when she travels. ____________
3. I do a lot of math mistakes. ____________
4. I fall in love of Emma Watson every time I see a photo of her. ____________
5. We get in trouble with being rude to our teachers. ____________



**3 Write sentences using the past simple.**

1. forget / her name / at the party
   I ____________________________________________
2. buy / a T-shirt / at the stadium
   My sister ____________________________________________
3. cell phone / get lost / during P.E. class
   His ____________________________________________
4. have fun / with our friends / yesterday
   We ____________________________________________
5. get in trouble / for / draw on the wall
   My brother ____________________________________________
6. make several mistakes / in my German homework
   I ____________________________________________
7. fall in love with / my new computer
   My friend ____________________________________________

## 4 Read and complete the text message.

dancing
eating
having
listening
losing
playing
talking
watching

Jan
online

Hi, we missed you at the party last night. You didn't miss much, it was really boring. I was with Lola the whole evening. I was (1) ______________ to her problems. She gets in trouble with her teachers all the time! Ed and Frank were (2) ______________ with the new girl from Denmark. She is very pretty, by the way. Elena and Lila were (3) ______________ incredible amounts of pizza—they seemed really hungry! Greg was (4) ______________ the football game on a big screen, but he wasn't (5) ______________ a good time. His team was (6) ______________. People weren't (7) ______________ because Eva was only (8) ______________ sad love songs. I think she is in love. Anyway, how are you?

Type a message



## 5 Read and circle the correct option.

1. I was sleeping **while / when** the earthquake started.
2. She was dancing **while / when** he was watching football.
3. My sister was playing with the dog **while / when** I was doing homework.
4. My parents were driving home **while / when** they heard the news.
5. I was thinking about her **while / when** I remembered it was her birthday.

## 6 Complete the sentences using the correct forms of the verbs.

rain run see start try

1. It was ____________________ while I was walking to the bus stop and I didn't have an umbrella!
2. Later, I was standing at the bus stop when I ____________________ a man with an enormous dog.
3. I was looking at the dog in admiration when suddenly it ____________________ barking at me.
4. The dog was pulling the man towards me while he was ____________________ behind him.
5. I was ____________________ to decide what to do when I realized it was my uncle Mack and the puppy I took care of last year during the summer. The puppy recognized me!

# Just for Fun

**1 In two minutes, find the following words in the unit and memorize the page number where each one appears. Then write the page numbers without looking.**

earthquake _____

lifeguards _____

neurons _____

reef _____

toy car _____

**2 In two minutes, scan the pages of the unit. Try to remember as many details as you can. Then answer the questions without looking.**

Who forgot his birthday? ____________________

What was Chief Brown drinking that morning? ____________________

Who was this man to the kids? ____________________

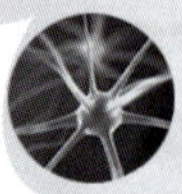
What is it? ____________________

What is the name of this rock? ____________________

**3 Read the story in pairs. Then follow the instructions to find out what happened.**

A lifeguard walked into a restaurant in a small town on the coast. The waiter was talking to a customer when he saw the lifeguard. He went over and asked him what he wanted to eat. The lifeguard said something to him quietly and asked only for a glass of water. He was waiting for the water, looking at the sea when he heard a noise and jumped. (The waiter threw the glass of water on the floor next to him and it broke.) The lifeguard smiled, said thank you and left.

a. Choose Student A and Student B.
b. Student A – go to page 158 and read the answer. Remember it.
c. Student B – ask Student A *Yes* / *No* questions.
d. Student B – just answer *Yes* or *No*.

**Examples of questions:**
Was the lifeguard hungry?
Did the lifeguard know the waiter?
Was the lifeguard feeling well?

6

# What do you need to travel?

# Vocabulary

**1** 25 **Listen and mark (✓) the vacation destination.**

1

a busy restaurant

an airport

2

a ski resort

a water park

3

a mountain trail

a beach

**2** 26 **Listen and number the activities.**

*The island of Santorini in Greece*

☐ book a flight

☐ exchange money

☐ get a passport

☐ pack a suitcase

☐ stay in a hotel

☐ hire a guide

☐ catch a train

**3** **Read the descriptions and write the travel activity.**

1. I went to a government office. I took some papers and two small photos. They gave me a small book with my personal information in it. ____________________
2. We used a computer to look at different schedules and prices. We used a credit card to pay, and they sent us an e-mail with our **itinerary**. ____________________
3. Two or three days before my trip, I started collecting clothing and items in a large rectangular bag. I hope I didn't forget anything! ____________________
4. We had money in dollars, but we were visiting France. We went to a place at the airport, gave them dollars and got euros back. ____________________
5. We looked for a name of a person who knew a lot about the places we wanted to visit. All the special restaurants and attractions. And the history! ____________________
6. I went to a large building near the beach. It had a beautiful swimming pool. I took my things to a room with a bed and a TV. I stayed there for four days. ____________________
7. Within France, we moved in a form of transportation that is slower than a plane, but you can see the landscape! ____________________

**Guess What!**
The most popular tourist destination in the world is France with 84 million visitors a year. The United States is in second place with 75 million visitors.

## 4 Read and match.

### Day 4 - Coyote Buttes, Utah

Today I hiked out to see "the wave" at Coyote Buttes. It's a beautiful rock formation in Utah. I got up at 5:30 to get ready: I packed plenty of water to drink—you get thirsty quickly in the desert—and a few snacks for when I get hungry. I put on comfortable clothes and hiking shoes. I wanted to get started before it got hot out, so I left the camp at 7:00. It took me six hours to get there because my GPS stopped working and I got lost. Fortunately, I found some other hikers who knew the way. Here's a photo of me looking at the site. It was amazing!

| | |
|---|---|
| 1. The Wave is | very early in the morning. |
| 2. The hiker woke up | helped him find the destination. |
| 3. To prepare, he | packed water and snacks. |
| 4. The trip took six hours | because he got lost in the desert. |
| 5. Some other hikers | a rock formation in Utah. |



## 5 Read again and underline the expressions with *get*. Then complete the dictionary entries.

1. **get** ______________: to become hot
2. **get** ______________: to want to eat food
3. **get** ______________: to not know where you are
4. **get** ______________: to prepare for something
5. **get** ______________: to begin an activity
6. **get** ______________: to arrive
7. **get** ______________: to want to drink water
8. **get** ______________: to wake up

3 min

## 6 Think Fast! Write five sentences using get.

1. ______________________________
2. ______________________________
3. ______________________________
4. ______________________________
5. ______________________________

**Glossary**

**reservation:** an arrangement to use a business' services

**itinerary:** a travel schedule

**GPS:** a device that identifies your exact location

# Grammar

**1** **Read and number the photos.**

Have you ever studied or lived in another country? Have you ever made friends from all over the world? The Jefferson International School has given this opportunity to thousands of students. It is located in the historic city of Lisbon, Portugal, and it offers a year abroad for high school students 16–18 years old.

* Please note: All applicants must pass an entrance exam.
For more information and applications contact: Eileen Powers, Admissions Officer epowers@jeffersoninternational.edu.pt

The program includes:

1. the opportunity to learn Portuguese
2. **room and board** with a Portuguese **host family**
3. personal tutor support
4. a variety of competitive sports programs (sailing, surfing, tennis, soccer, swimming and basketball)
5. trips to cultural landmarks in Portugal and Spain

**2** **Complete the e-mail.**

heard a lot of | I am studying | program at Jefferson
My cousin did a | send me | to Portugal before

Untitled

MESSAGE OPTIONS

To: Eileen Powers <epowers@jeffersoninternational.edu.pt>
Cc: Francesca Rossi <francesca.rossi15@email.com.it>
Subject: Application to Jefferson International School

Dear Ms. Powers,

I am interested in the study abroad (1) ______________ International School. I'm Italian and am 16 years old. At the moment, (2) ______________ at the Liceo Garibaldi in Milan. I haven't been (3) ______________, but I have taken Portuguese lessons for a year.

I have (4) ______________ good things about studying abroad. (5) ______________ study abroad program recently, and she has had a wonderful experience.

Can you please (6) ______________ an application for the program?

Sincerely,

Francesca Rossi

### Present Perfect

We use *have* with past participles to talk about the present results of past actions:

She **has had** a wonderful experience.

I **haven't been** to Portugal.

### Guess What!

We use the present perfect and *ever* to ask about life experiences: **Have** you **ever been** to England?

### Glossary

**room and board:** a place to live and meals to eat

**host family:** a family that invites a person to stay in their home

**scholarship:** free tuition offered by a school or university

## Present Perfect: *Already*, *Yet*

We use *already* with the present perfect for an event that has occurred:
He **has already made** some friends.
We use *yet* with questions and negative forms:
**Have** you **seen** anything interesting **yet**?
I **haven't gone** to any museums **yet**.

**3** **Write the past participles of the verbs. Use the ad and the e-mail on page 86.**

1. study ______________________
2. live ______________________
3. make ______________________
4. give ______________________
5. be ______________________
6. take ______________________
7. hear ______________________
8. have ______________________

**4** **Complete the sentences using the present perfect.**

1. I ______________________ (*be*) to Norway and Denmark.
2. She ______________________ (*hear*) about a program in Chile.
3. He ______________________ (*live*) with a host family before.
4. The school ______________________ (*give*) **scholarships** to fifteen international students.

5 min

**5** **Think Fast!** In your notebook, write the past simple forms of the verbs in Activity 3.

**6** 27 **Listen and mark (✓) the correct option.**



Home
Contacts
Recent
Jo

☆ Jason
Online

1. Who is Jason?
   - [ ] Jo's friend
   - [ ] Jo's cousin
2. How old is Jo?
   - [ ] 16
   - [ ] 17
3. Has Jo learned some Portuguese?
   - [ ] Yes, he has.
   - [ ] No, he hasn't.
4. Has he seen anything interesting yet?
   - [ ] Yes, he has.
   - [ ] No, he hasn't.
5. What has he done?
   - [ ] visited St. George's Castle
   - [ ] tried some unusual foods

**7** 27 **Listen again and complete using *already* or *yet*.**

1. Have you learned Portuguese ______________________?
2. I've ______________________ learned a few expressions.
3. Have you made any friends ______________________?
4. Have you seen anything interesting ______________________?
5. I've ______________________ tried some unusual foods.

# Reading & Listening

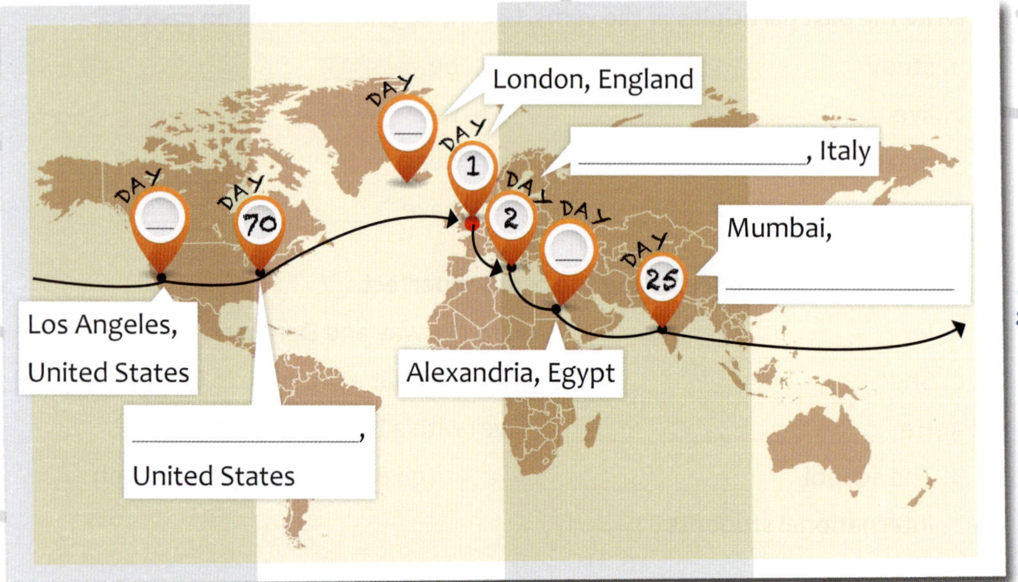


**Be Strategic!** Photos, maps and infographics can give clues to the type of information in a text and how it is organized.

**1 Look at the map and mark (✓) the correct option.**

1. This article probably lists...
   - ☐ possible destinations for a future vacation.
   - ☐ destinations in a trip around the world.
   - ☐ modern forms of ocean transportation.

88

2. The information is probably organized...
   - ☐ in chronological order.
   - ☐ as a main point with supporting ideas.

**2 Scan and complete the information on the map.**

## Around the World in 80 Days

1 In Jules Verne's popular **novel** *Around the World in 80 Days*, the main character, Phileas Fogg, **makes a bet** that he can travel around the world in 80 days. Because the story takes place in the nineteenth century, Phileas Fogg can only travel using transportation from that time period, such as boats and trains. While nowadays you can travel around the world in a few days, 80 days was once an impressive accomplishment. Phileas Fogg's fictional adventures have captured readers' imaginations for almost 150 years, but this story doesn't end there.

2 Michael Palin is a famous world traveler. He does travel programs for the BBC. His first program, also called *Around the World in 80 Days*, was based on Jules Verne's novel. Michael Palin traveled around the world in 80 days using Fogg's route and nineteenth-century forms of transportation.

3 Michael's **journey** started in London on a train **bound for** Italy. By Day 2, he was in Venice. From there he traveled by boat to Athens, and from Athens across the Mediterranean Sea. He reached Alexandria, Egypt on Day 7. In Egypt, he traveled by train and camel, and boarded a boat going to India. He arrived in Mumbai, India on Day 25. From there, he took a train and arrived in Madras on Day 29. He crossed the Indian Ocean by boat, arriving in Singapore on Day 38, Shanghai, China on Day 46 and Yokohama, Japan on Day 50. From there, he crossed the Pacific Ocean to Los Angeles. He arrived on Day 64. He traveled by train across the United States to get to New York on Day 70. Finally, he sailed across the Atlantic Ocean to reach his final destination in London on Day 79. He traveled more than 45,000 kilometers.

### Glossary

**novel:** a fiction book

**make a bet:** to arrange to pay someone if you guess something incorrectly, or for a person to pay you if you guess something correctly

**journey:** travel over a large distance

**bound for:** going to a specific place

**3** **Write *1, 2* or *3* to indicate the correct paragraph.**

1. This paragraph is a description of Michael Palin's trip. ______
2. This paragraph gives background information on Michael Palin. ______
3. This paragraph gives information in chronological order. ______
4. This paragraph introduces the book *Around the World in 80 Days*. ______

**4** **Read and circle *T* (True) or *F* (False).**

1. Phileas Fogg lived 150 years ago. T F
2. Jules Verne wrote *Around the World in 80 Days*. T F
3. Michael followed the same route as Phileas Fogg. T F
4. He used modern forms of transportation. T F
5. He traveled from Greece to Italy. T F
6. It took 64 days to reach Japan. T F
7. Michael's journey took less than 80 days. T F

**5** 28 **Listen and number the photos.**

**6** 28 **Listen again and circle the correct option.**

1. What exactly is virtual **travel** / **reality**?
2. If you turn your **head** / **headset**, the image moves.
3. Some governments make **simulations** / **virtual tours** of famous landmarks.
4. But can you **find** / **buy** one of these devices?
5. You can **turn** / **make** your phone into a virtual reality device…

**Stop and Think!** What are the advantages and disadvantages of virtual travel?

**Glossary**

**headset:** a device you wear on your head

**simulation:** a re-creation of specific circumstances, often for training

**relive:** experience something again

**cardboard:** thick paper, often brown and used for boxes

# Culture

**1 Read and match.**

| | |
|---|---|
| 1. Sri Lanka is a small island | is volleyball. |
| 2. The country has the oldest | in the Indian Ocean. |
| 3. Cinnamon, a popular spice, | rice and curry. |
| 4. Sri Lanka is the world's largest | flag in the world. |
| 5. The national sport of Sri Lanka | exporter of tea. |
| 6. A popular Sri Lankan dish is | originated in Sri Lanka. |

**2 Read and mark (✓) the correct option.**

## ❮Shipwreck Diving❯

The country of Sri Lanka has a unique geographical position along one of the world's major shipping routes from East to West. For hundreds of years, ships have sailed this route. Many of these ships have sunk near the Sri Lankan coast because of storms, bad navigation and wars. Today, there are over 200 shipwrecks off the coast of Sri Lanka—and many are **unexplored**. Some of the wrecks are easy for **divers** to reach—only 30 or 40 meters below the surface—and the water is very clear. For this reason, shipwreck diving has become a popular tourist activity in Sri Lanka. After a three-day diving course, tourists can dive to see a real shipwreck.

What can you see when you dive to a shipwreck? Marine life. When a ship sinks, coral starts to cover the structure. Other creatures and fish follow, creating an artificial coral reef. For divers, the experience of diving down to the wreck and seeing the different plants and fish is **unforgettable**.

Visiting a shipwreck is also an excellent way to experience history. Many of the ships have fascinating stories. For example, marine archaeologists have discovered a wreck off the town of Godavaya. It's over 2,000 years old and full of ancient artifacts. Another shipwreck is the *HMS Hermes*, the world's first **aircraft carrier**. It sank in 1942 during the Second World War. It is in excellent condition, and it is very popular with divers.

Unfortunately, shipwrecks are also in danger. Some people visit the shipwrecks to salvage metal: they use explosives to cut apart ships, so that they can sell the metal. This destroys the marine environment,kills the fish there, and erases history. ▼

To learn more about Sri Lanka's shipwrecks, go to www.divesrilanka.com

**Guess What!**
The official capital of Sri Lanka is Sri Jayawardenapura Kotte, or Kotte for short. It is near the city of Colombo, the business capital of the country.

1. There are a lot of shipwrecks off the coast of Sri Lanka because...
   - ☐ the currents near the island are dangerous.
   - ☐ the island is near a major shipping route.
2. Shipwrecks have become a popular attraction because...
   - ☐ they are easy for divers to reach.
   - ☐ there are sharks and whales near the wrecks.
3. Shipwrecks are a great place to view...
   - ☐ ancient temples and artifacts.
   - ☐ coral, fish and other marine life.
4. Some people visit the shipwrecks because...
   - ☐ they are interested in history.
   - ☐ they want to become better divers.
5. Shipwrecks are in danger because...
   - ☐ people salvage metal from the wrecks.
   - ☐ violent storms are destroying the wrecks.

**3** 29 **Listen and complete the notes.**

Description of an Auto Rickshaw

- ________________ wheels
- metal body and **canvas roof**

________________ passengers

Advantages of Auto Rickshaws

- ________________ than a car
- ________________ enough for **narrow** country roads
- works well in ________________

Disadvantages of Auto Rickshaws

- not ________________
- cause ________________
- make a lot of noise

**4 Read and answer. What do people in Sri Lanka call auto rickshaws?**

________________________________________

**Stop and Think!** What adventurous activities can world travelers do in your country?

## Glossary

**unexplored:** not explored

**divers:** people who go under water, often with special equipment

**unforgettable:** very memorable; you cannot forget it

**aircraft carrier:** a military ship that carries airplanes

**canvas:** strong waterproof fabric

**roof:** the covering of a house or vehicle

**narrow:** not wide

# Project

**1 Look and classify the activities for each destination.**

swim in the ocean

sail

find a treasure

ride horses

mine for gold

stay at a five star hotel

1. A Tropical Beach

______________________

______________________

☐

2. The Old West

______________________

______________________

☐

3. A Pirate Ship

______________________

______________________

☐



**2 30 Listen and mark (✓) the destination.**

**3 Look at the Travel Experience poster on page 93. What is the destination?**

☐ A ski resort in the Alps
☐ A jousting tournament in the Middle Ages
☐ A city in the ancient Roman Empire

**4 Read and circle the correct option.**

1. The destination is **real** / **historical** / **fictional**.
2. The main event is a **tour of secret tunnels** / **jousting tournament**.
3. The poster gives **one example** / **two examples** of foods to eat.
4. The poster **mentions** / **doesn't mention** where visitors will stay.

**5 Design a Travel Experience poster.**

1. Choose a destination. It can be a real place like New Zealand, a historical setting like ancient Rome or even a fictional place like Middle Earth from *Lord of the Rings*.
2. Research the destination. Pick a main attraction for travelers to experience: What can visitors see or do at that attraction?
3. Plan food and accommodations: What will travelers eat? Where will they stay?
4. Make a poster and present your travel experience to the class.

# Visit Medieval England! Enjoy a Jousting Tournament!

Jousting—so exciting!

Secret tunnels!

A turkey leg! Mmm!

Knight's armor!

Jousting was a popular sport in Europe in the Middle Ages. If you go back to the 1100s, you can attend a jousting tournament. When you arrive, you will stay at our luxury accommodations in Dover Castle! It is one of the largest castles in England. Eat in the Great Hall in the presence of the King Henry II. Don't forget to bring a knife—forks won't become popular for two hundred years! But don't worry! If you forget, another guest might share his with you. Or just eat a big turkey leg! Before the tournament, you will have time to explore the secret tunnels around Dover Castle. But save some energy for the main event: there is a lot to see at the tournament. Watch colorful processions with flags and trumpet players. Listen to musicians sing and tell stories. For jousting, knights ride horses and wear heavy, metal armor. They try to hit each other with long lances. It's a dangerous sport, but very exciting to see!

Dover Castle!

Musicians in costumes!

Colorful processions!

# Review

**1 Look and complete the travel activities.**

1

__________________ a flight

4

__________________ a passport

2

__________________ a train

5

__________________ a guide

3

__________________ in a hotel

6

__________________ money

7

__________________ a suitcase

## 2 Look and circle the correct option.

get hot / get hungry

get there / get lost

get started / get thirsty

get up / get ready

## 3 Look and write the past participle form of the verbs.

eat – ____________________

make – ____________________

take – ____________________

give – ____________________

hear – ____________________

see – ____________________

## 4 Unscramble the sentences.

1. has / Bryan / Japan / been / to ____________________
2. for / studied / the / Karen / hasn't / test ____________________
3. ever / letter / you / a / have / written / ? ____________________
4. have / gone / to / ever / you / concert / a / ? ____________________

## 5 Look and write the sentences using the present perfect.

1. we / have lunch / already

____________________

2. she / not be / to the museum / yet

____________________

3. he / take / the test / already

____________________

4. they / not see / the movie / yet

____________________

5. you / do / your chores / yet / ?

____________________

# Just for Fun

**1 Find and circle eight words that form expressions with *get*.**

hot hungry lost ready started there thirsty up

N D F O T V T J Y T Q X D Z G Y
F A U K H Q H U N H Y H L F X R
S H L B I I E W E T P J O B H G
T L L G R L R J X B R Z C T H N
A O F R S X E D D R E J B V F U
R S F U T E Y E E Q A G B R Q H
T T Z B Y R R K I C D T I R E D
E Y S K G O I R A O Y Q W I W C
D Q O N B X Y U P L Q A N G R Y

**2 Find six new words that form expressions with *get*. Then complete.**

get...

1

a___gry

2

b___r___d

3

c___ ___d

4

f___ ___l

5

t___ ___ed

6

w___t

7

# How adventurous are you?

# Vocabulary

**1** [31] **Listen and number the extreme sports.**

rock climbing

kite surfing

snowboarding

mountain biking

skydiving

white water rafting

**2** **Look and write the name of the extreme sport.**

1

______________________

2

______________________

3

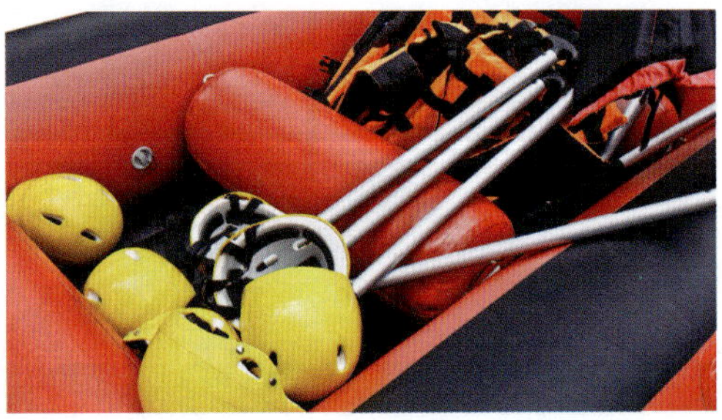

______________________

4

______________________

5

______________________

6

______________________

**3** 31 **Listen again and complete.**

boring exciting interesting terrifying thrilling tiring

1. It's really ______________ —your heart beats fast and you forget about everything else.
2. You see a lot of ______________ places when you go mountain biking.
3. It's never ______________. Every mountain is different.
4. My mom thinks skydiving is ______________... She's extremely afraid of heights.
5. It's ______________ to be in the middle of a river navigating the currents.
6. You have to train a lot because climbing can be very ______________.

3 min **4 Think Fast!** **Describe the extreme sports using the adjectives in Activity 3.**

*I think white water rafting is terrifying. I'm afraid of water.*

**5 Look and label.**

bored excited interested terrified thrilled tired

1. ______________ 2. ______________ 3. ______________ 4. ______________ 5. ______________ 6. ______________

**6 Read and match.**

1. Jo is bored because
2. He's excited because
3. He's interested in
4. He's terrified of
5. He's thrilled about
6. He's tired because

his favorite team is winning.
a new book from the library.
winning a sports car!
he's waiting in a long line.
he did a lot of chores.
a giant spider.

3 min **7 Think Fast!** **Complete the table.**

| boring | | interesting | | thrilling | |
|---|---|---|---|---|---|
| | excited | | terrified | | tired |

# Grammar

1 [32] **Look at the Wild Adventures Survival Courses brochure. Then listen and circle *T* (True) or *F* (False).**

| | | |
|---|---|---|
| 1. Tyler has already taken a survival course. | T | F |
| 2. Megan is taking the Jungle Explorer course this year. | T | F |
| 3. Tyler hasn't decided which course to take. | T | F |
| 4. He might take the Mountain Adventurer course. | T | F |
| 5. Megan recommends the Island Survivor course. | T | F |
| 6. Megan definitely can't take a course this year. | T | F |

2 **Read and mark (✓) about you. Then calculate your Survival IQ.**

## Survival IQ

**1** Would you eat a **bug**?

☐ Yes, I would. ☐ I might. ☐ No, I wouldn't.

In Western countries, people often think bugs are disgusting, but in other parts of the world, people eat them every day. They're very high in protein. Go ahead and take a bite! Just make sure you know which bugs are safe to eat!

+ = 25 points +/– = 15 points – = 5 points

**2** Would you drink water from a lake or river?

☐ Yes, I would. ☐ I might. ☐ No, I wouldn't.

If you are lost in the forest, or worse—in the desert—your most important resource is clean water. You should always carry water when you go hiking. Don't drink from a lake or river. It might have dangerous bacteria or parasites that could make you very sick.

+ = 5 points +/– = 10 points – = 25 points

## Wild Adventures Survival Courses

### Junior Survivor

Difficulty Level: All

Ages: 8 – 15

Learn how to have fun, stay safe and protect the forest.

### Island Survivor

Difficulty Level: All

Ages: 12 and up

Learn survival skills on an **uninhabited** tropical island! Find fresh water, catch fish and build a fire.

### Mountain Adventurer

Difficulty Level: Experienced

Ages: 15 and up

Practice your survival skills in the mountains! Find out which plants are safe to eat, build a waterproof shelter and cook fresh **game** over a fire.

### Jungle Explorer

Difficulty Level: Expert

Ages: 18 and up

Survive a trip through the jungle. Use trees and plants to construct a **raft** and then navigate through the jungle on white water **rapids**.

### *Might*

We use the modal *might* before verbs to indicate possibility:

I **might** take the Island Survivor course.

The negative form also indicates possibility:

I **might not** sign up this year.

## 3 Would you run away from a bear?

☐ Yes, I would. ☐ I might. ☐ No, I wouldn't.

Actually, running from a bear is a terrible idea. Why? Because bears can run faster than you can. They can also climb trees. If you see a bear, or any other large animal, you should try to scare the animal: shout, jump and wave your arms. If you're lucky, the animal will run away.

+ = 0 points +/– = 0 points – = 25 points

## 4 Would you eat wild berries?

☐ Yes, I would. ☐ I might. ☐ No, I wouldn't.

Imagine that you're in the forest and you haven't eaten in two days. You see some delicious-looking red berries. What do you do? If you aren't 100% certain that they're safe to eat, you should not eat them. Some berries are very toxic.

+ = 10 points +/– = 20 points – = 25 points

## 5 Would you take a compass and a map?

☐ Yes, I would! ☐ I might. ☐ No, I wouldn't.

Nowadays, with maps on our phones and GPS trackers, you might want to leave the compass and paper map at home. That is a bad idea. Devices can get wet, broken or lost. If you are in the wilderness, you need a compass and a map to navigate, and you should know how to use them.

+ = 25 points +/– = 15 points – = 5 points

**Would**

**Would** you eat a bug?
Yes, I **would**!
No, I **wouldn't**.

**Scores:**
**125 points:** You're a Survival Genius! You know some important facts to stay safe in nature.
**85 – 120 points:** Not too bad… Maybe you should take a survival course.
**25 – 80 points:** You should explore nature more, but take an experienced guide with you!



**3** 🎧[33] **Listen and mark (✓ or ✗) the activities that each person has done.**

go bungee jumping ☐

swim with sharks ☐

touch a spider ☐

see a tornado ☐

**Present Perfect: *Never***

I've **never** been very adventurous.
He's **never gone** skydiving.

**4** **Write sentences about Tara and Mike using the present perfect.**

1. ______________________
2. ______________________
3. ______________________
4. ______________________

2 min **5** **Think Fast! In your notebook, write four sentences about things you have never done.**

**Glossary**

**uninhabited:** with no people living there
**game:** wild animals that you eat
**raft:** a simple boat
**rapids:** a part of a river with rocks and strong currents
**bug:** an insect

# Reading & Writing

**Be Strategic!**
Understanding text organization can make you a better reader *and* writer. Each paragraph is a category of information. If you can classify information, you can write a clear, organized text.

**1 Look and classify the words.**

tiger school scared sad face lion supermarket angry elephant museum hands arms zebra library happy feet

Zoo Animals

______
______
______
______

City Places

______
______
______
______

Emotions

______
______
______
______

Body Parts

______
______
______
______

**2 Read and number the headings.**

☐ Animals as Transportation ☐ Technology and Transportation ☐ The **Roots** of Human Exploration

## Animals and Adventure

1 Modern technology has improved transportation and our ability to explore. We can send **space probes** to distant planets and submarines to the deepest parts of the ocean. We can zoom around the world on planes and high-speed trains. Buses and subways carry commuters through cities, and cars take us to our many destinations—even without humans driving them!

2 Just a century ago, transportation often involved animals. **Oxen** pulled farmers' **plows** and wagons. Horses carried people from place to place. **Mules** pulled canal boats and mine cars full of coal. But they weren't the only animals used for transportation. Travelers have used camels, ideally suited for the desert, for hundreds of years. Some call them "ships of the desert." In India and Thailand, elephants were useful for transportation, while in the arctic, dogs and reindeer pulled sleds in the snow.

3 Long before humans used animals as transportation, animals influenced human migration. In fact, this might be the reason why humans became so adventurous. For thousands of years, across Africa, Asia, Europe and the Americas, humans followed the animals that were their food: fish, buffalo, bison—even mammoths. Later, humans developed agriculture, but they still moved with their animals—sheep, goats and cattle—across plains and deserts. The cowboys herded cattle from the American West to railroad towns to feed cities across the country. Animals are still an important part of transportation in some places, and if you have the opportunity to explore, you might get to see a dog sled or ride an elephant. Just remember that you probably have animals to thank for being an adventurer in the first place.

**3 Read again. Underline names of working animals and circle names of food animals.**

**4 Imagine you need to add facts to the article. Circle the correct option.**

| | | | |
|---|---|---|---|
| 1. helicopters | Paragraph 1 | Paragraph 2 | Paragraph 3 |
| 2. horses that carried soldiers | Paragraph 1 | Paragraph 2 | Paragraph 3 |
| 3. the first humans in North America | Paragraph 1 | Paragraph 2 | Paragraph 3 |
| 4. travel to the moon | Paragraph 1 | Paragraph 2 | Paragraph 3 |

**5 Classify the facts for an article about sled dogs. Write *B* (Basic Facts) or *H* (History).**

1. Huskies and malamutes are the most common breeds of sled dog. _____
2. People started using dog sleds 3,000 years ago in arctic regions. _____
3. Dog sleds were the main form of winter transportation until the mid 20th century. _____
4. Dogs traveled from northern Asia to North America with humans. _____
5. Sled dogs can run 30 km per hour. _____
6. Their favorite food is reindeer meat. _____

**6 In your notebook, write two paragraphs about sled dogs using the facts in Activity 5.**

**Stop and Think!** Is it OK to use animals for food and/or work? Why or why not?

## Glossary

**roots:** the parts of a plant in soil; the origins of a person or thing

**space probes:** machines that collect information in space

**oxen:** two or more cows that pull a wagon or farm equipment

**plows:** farm equipment for digging and moving soil

**mules:** working animals; a combination of a horse and a donkey

# Culture



**1** 34 **Read and guess. Then listen and circle the correct option.**

1. Antarctica is in the **northern** / **southern** hemisphere.
2. Antarctica is **half** / **twice** the size of Australia.
3. Most of the continent is covered in 1.6 kilometers of **snow** / **ice**.
4. Antarctica is the world's largest **desert** / **island**.
5. **Summer** / **Winter** in Antarctica begins in December.
6. Around **1,000** / **4,000** people—mostly scientists—live in Antarctica in the summer months.
7. In the winter, it is **sunny** / **dark** for 24 hours a day.

**2** **Look and label the map.**

- Africa
- Australia
- Atlantic Ocean
- Indian Ocean
- Pacific Ocean
- South America

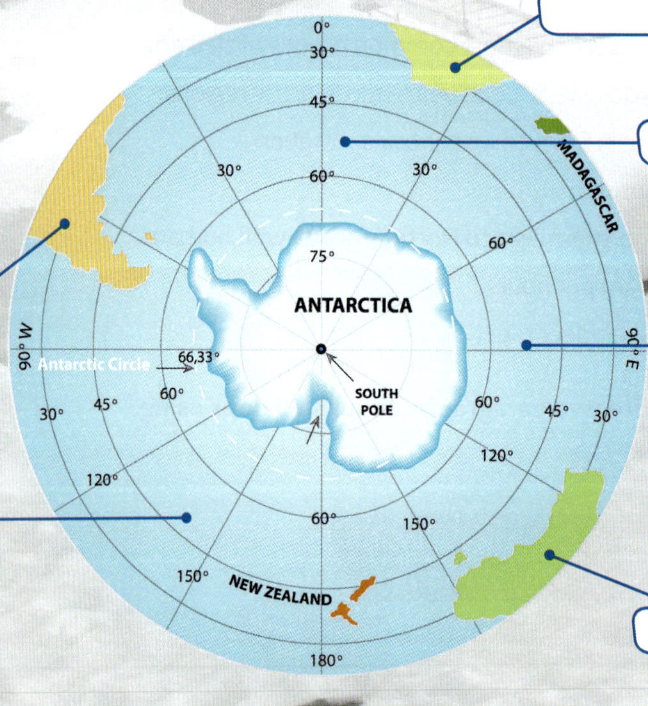

**3** **Read the article and write *A* (Amundsen) or *S* (Scott).**

## The Race to the South Pole

In 1910, two teams of explorers set out on the **ultimate** adventure to become the first people to **reach** the South Pole. It was a very dangerous trip. The total distance to the South Pole and back to safety was nearly 3,000 kilometers. They needed to cross mountains and glaciers, and the average temperature was around -30°C.

One team was led by Roald Amundsen, a Norwegian explorer. Amundsen learned about arctic survival from Inuit people, and other team members had experience living in extreme arctic conditions. They planned to use skis and dog sleds to travel across Antarctica to reach the South Pole.

The other team was led by Robert F. Scott, a British captain who had explored Antarctica in an earlier expedition. His plan was to use mostly horses and **motorized** sleds to get to the South Pole.

Amundsen's team set out for the South Pole on October 20, 1911, and they arrived on December 14th. They returned safely to their base camp on January 26, 1912.

Scott's team set out November 1, 1911. They struggled with the horses and the motorized sleds, but they did reach the South Pole on January 17, 1912. They found a tent full of **supplies** and a note from Amundsen. They were not the first team at the South Pole! **Tragically**, on the return trip, the temperatures dropped to -40°C and they all died in a snowstorm only 18 kilometers from their base camp.

Robert F. Scott and his team were seen as great heroes. The scientific research from Scott's Terra Nova Expedition established Antarctica as a research site for many different areas of study including geology, biology and meteorology.

105

1. He led two Antarctic expeditions. ____
2. He was British. ____
3. He was Norwegian. ____
4. He was familiar with Inuit survival skills. ____
5. He used skis and dog sleds. ____
6. He used horses and motorized sleds. ____
7. He was first to reach the South Pole. ____
8. He led the Terra Nova Expedition. ____

**4** **Underline the dates in the article. Then complete the timeline.**

Amundsen sets out ____

Amundsen reaches the South Pole ____

Amundsen reaches base camp ____

Scott sets out ____

Scott reaches the South Pole ____

**Stop and Think!** Is it OK for people to risk their lives in order to explore a place? Why or why not?

**Glossary**

**ultimate:** the best

**reach:** to arrive at

**motorized:** with a motor

**supplies:** necessary items, often food

**tragically:** sadly

# Project

**1** **Look at the Adventure Profile on page 107. What was the adventure?**

**2** **Read and underline the Adventure Profile facts in the article.**

After high school, many young people wait a year before going to college. Some work, some volunteer and some travel. Tom Davies, a nineteen-year-old from London, decided to cycle around the world!

To prepare, Tom spent several months training. He did a lot of exercise in the gym and also rode his bicycle on difficult terrains. He was very careful about which items to pack. He couldn't take many things, just some clothing, a phone, a laptop and a repair kit for his bike. He didn't take a tent. He planned to stay in hotels. (His parents helped with the expenses.)

For the first part of his trip, Tom went through France, Italy, Albania and Greece all the way to Istanbul, in Turkey. Then he flew to Mumbai and cycled across India. His next stop was Myanmar, and then Vietnam. From there, he cycled to Thailand and Singapore. He flew to Australia to cycle across the country and after that, New Zealand. He flew to San Francisco, in the United States, and cycled north to Canada. He flew to Spain, then cycled north through France, home to London.

Tom Davies cycled a total of 46,620 kilometers in 174 days. Most of the journey went well, but he did have a few challenges: food poisoning in Italy, bad weather, being chased by dogs in Albania and a group of monkeys in India. Tom became the youngest person to cycle around the world and he raised $80,000 for charity.



**3** 35 **Listen and circle the correct option.**

Adventurer: **Jonathan / Jessica** Meir

Age: **28 / 38** years old

Transportation: spacecraft

Distance: 54.6 **million / billion** kilometers

Places: the US, France, **Korea / Canada**, Antarctica, Belize

Preparation: astronaut training, learning **Japanese / Russian**

Challenges: living in a dangerous environment, being away from family

Achievements: She has become a marine biologist, a pilot and an **artist / astronaut**.

Future Plans: She plans to accept any mission NASA gives her. She might be one of the first humans on **the Moon / Mars**.

**4** **Choose and research an adventurer. Make an Adventure Profile.**

Laura Dekker | Jordan Romero | Jade Hameister | Dashiel Alsup | Trinity Arsenault

# ADVENTURE PROFILE

**NAME:** Tom Davies

**AGE:** 19 years old

**PLACES VISITED:** France, Italy, Albania, Greece, Turkey, India, Myanmar, Vietnam, Thailand, Singapore, Australia, New Zealand, the US, Canada, Spain

**TRANSPORTATION:** bicycle, airplane

**TRAVEL DISTANCE:** 46,620 kilometers

**PREPARATION ACTIVITIES:** exercising, riding his bike on difficult terrain

**CHALLENGES:** food poisoning, bad weather, dogs, monkeys

**ACHIEVEMENTS:** He was the youngest person to cycle around the world. He raised $80,000 for charity.

# Review

## 1 Look and label the extreme sports.

1 
_______________

2 
_______________

3 
_______________

4 
_______________

5 
_______________

6 
_______________

## 2 Read and circle the correct option.

1. The movie about the vampire was **terrified / terrifying**.
2. We were very **tired / tiring** after we did all of our chores.
3. The hot air balloon trip was **thrilled / thrilling**!
4. 108 The children were **excited / exciting** about their visit to the zoo.
5. I was **bored / boring** waiting for my flight, so I read a magazine.
6. I read an **interested / interesting** article about hiking in Europe.

## 3 Complete the sentences using the unused words from Activity 2.

1. The new action movie was _______________. You should see it!
2. To apply for the scholarship, you need to complete a lot of _______________ forms.
3. Cycling across the country was very _______________. Next time, I'm flying!
4. He was _______________ when his parents gave him a new car.
5. My brother is really _______________ in Manga.
6. My mom was _______________ when she saw a mouse in the kitchen.

## 4 Read and correct the sentences.

1. I might going to the gym this afternoon.
_______________________________________________
2. We might not to go to the party tomorrow.
_______________________________________________
3. My family is might travel to Spain this summer.
_______________________________________________
4. She might has basketball practice after school.
_______________________________________________

## 5 Look and write the questions using *would*. Then answer about you.

1 

ride in an auto rickshaw

________________________________________

Yes, I would. No, I wouldn't.

2 

eat street food

________________________________________

Yes, I would. No, I wouldn't.

3 

go on a cruise

________________________________________

Yes, I would. No, I wouldn't.

4 

drink yak's milk

________________________________________

Yes, I would. No, I wouldn't.

## 6 Look and write about Gianna and Quinn using the present perfect and *never*.

| | | win a race | take a dance class | fail a test | go sailing | fly in a plane |
|---|---|---|---|---|---|---|
|  | Gianna | ✓ | ✓ | ✗ | ✗ | ✓ |
|  | Quinn | ✗ | ✗ | ✓ | ✓ | ✓ |

1. ________________________________________
2. ________________________________________
3. ________________________________________
4. ________________________________________

# Just for Fun

**1** **Look and write the extreme sports.**

1 

______________________

2 

______________________

3 

______________________

4 

______________________

5 

______________________

6 

______________________

**2** **Look and complete.**



| | | | | |
|---|---|---|---|---|
|  | exciting | excite | ______ |  |
|  | ______ | terrify | ______ |  |
|  | boring | bore | ______ |  |
|  | ______ | thrill | thrilled |  |
|  | interesting | interest | ______ |  |
|  | ______ | tire | tired |  |

8

# What do we have in common?

# Vocabulary

**1** 🎧[36] **Listen and write *J* (Jaya), *B* (Bryan) or *M* (Maia). Which activities do they do?**

➤ 112

**2** 🎧[36] **Listen again and circle the correct option.**

1. Jaya streams movies or TV series with her **brother** / **sister** Adya.
2. They do that on **weekends** / **weekdays**.
3. Bryan plays **basketball** / **football** with his friends.
4. To work out, he **lifts weights** / **goes jogging**.
5. Maia loves ordering **Mexican** / **Chinese** take-out.
6. On the weekends, she sleeps in until **ten** / **eleven** o'clock.

## 4 Read the blog and write the headings.

A Big Move!  I'm on the Team!  Whew! A Long Week

david.blogspot.com

### September 12th – ____________

It's hard to believe it, but I've been here for three weeks. The time has passed really fast and I've already made some friends. Classes are going well, and I'm starting to feel like I know my way around. This school is different from my old school because it's very diverse. There are kids from Asia, Latin America and Africa. One of my best friends is from Somalia. His name is Nadif! And… Soccer tryouts went great! I just found out that I'm on the soccer team. Practice starts this week!

By David | 5 Comments | Read More ›

### August 29th – ____________

I just finished my first week at my new school. Things are going well. I miss my old friends, but people here are OK. Since I'm a new student, the school assigned me a partner—Jarred—and he's helping me **get used to** the school. Some kids started making fun of my red hair. It wasn't a big deal, but Jarred and some of his friends told them to stop. And one of my classmates invited me to her birthday party this weekend. It'll be a good chance to meet some people!

By David | 1 Comments | Read More ›

### July 27th – ____________

Well, it's official: I'm going to a new school in the fall. My dad has a new job and we're moving to a different city. The good thing is my sister is going to the same school, so at least I'll know someone. Yesterday I said good-bye to my friends. We agreed to keep in touch. It shouldn't be too hard with social media, but it's not the same as being there. I saw the webpage for the new school and it looks good. They have a soccer team. I can't wait for **tryouts**. My sister wants to play volleyball. I'm excited, but a little nervous.

**David Wells**

Search

FOLLOW US

## 5 Read and circle T (True) or F (False).

1. David moved to a different country. T F
2. His sister is going to college. T F
3. He looked at the school's webpage. T F
4. Everyone has treated David well. T F
5. Jarred doesn't have any friends. T F
6. The school is very diverse. T F
7. David's new best friend is from Africa. T F
8. Soccer practice starts soon. T F

**Stop and Think!** How can friendship prevent bullying?

### Glossary

**physical:** involving the body or real objects

**stuff:** things

**exclude:** to not allow someone to participate

**tryouts:** a test of abilities in order to be on a team

**get used to:** to get accustomed to; to adapt

# Culture

**1** **Read and number the photos.**

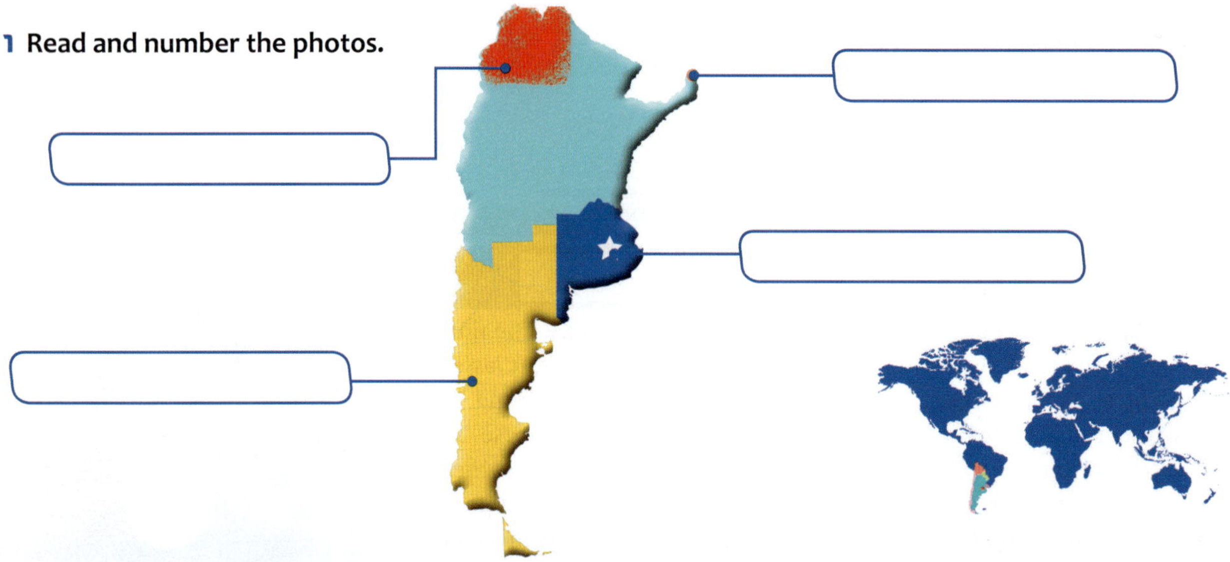

## Argentina

There are many different places that make up the country of Argentina. Argentina has the Andes Mountains in the west and the Atlantic Ocean along the eastern coast. It stretches 3,694 kilometers from north to south.

1. Iguazu Falls is located in the north of Argentina on the border with Brazil. There are 275 individual waterfalls! The falls are a part of a jungle ecosystem.
2. Patagonia is an area in the south of Argentina and the neighboring country of Chile. Not a lot of people live there, but many people visit to see its snowy mountain landscapes.
3. The northeast region of Argentina is a high **altitude** desert called the Puna de Atacama. Many people go rock climbing there.
4. The capital city, Buenos Aires, is in the east of the country. It is on the Atlantic Coast near Uruguay.

**2** **Read again and label the map.**

**3** 40 **Read and guess. Then listen and circle the correct option.**

1. There are **penguins** / **turtles** in Argentina.
2. Argentina means "**Country** / **Land** of Silver."
3. *Gauchos* are Argentinean **cowboys** / **boots**.
4. *Yerba mate* is a traditional **drink** / **food**.
5. **The tango** / **Salsa** is a dance from Argentina.
6. *Dulce de leche* is made with milk and **salt** / **sugar**.

## 4 Read and complete the text.

became
groups
important
introduced
like
million
others
people
President
stores

When the Spanish came to the Americas in the 16th century, they brought (1) ________________ from Spain to live in Argentina. These new settlers added to the indigenous peoples of the region. When the country (2) ________________ independent in 1818, more Europeans came to Argentina. There were immigrants from Spain, Italy, France, Germany and Britain. (3) ________________ came from Russia and Eastern Europe. Many Jewish people came to Argentina to escape **persecution**. The population jumped from only four (4) ________________ in 1895 to 16 million just fifty years later. This was not an accident. In fact, the government of Argentina invited immigrants to the country because there was a lot of land and not many people.

Argentina has a very unique culture because of all of these immigrants. Italian foods (5) ________________ pasta and pizza are an (6) ________________ part of Argentinean **cuisine**. British immigrants built railways and (7) ________________ the sport of soccer. There is even a region in Argentina now where people speak Welsh. There was also a (8) ________________ of Argentina—Carlos Menem—whose parents were Syrian immigrants! Even the accent of Argentinean Spanish is a result of the many different immigrant (9) ________________. Nowadays, there are many immigrants from Asia. There are neighborhoods in Buenos Aires where you can find authentic Chinese and Korean restaurants and (10) ________________. Immigration continues to **enrich** and transform the country.

## 5 Read and match.

| | |
|---|---|
| 1. The Spanish were | was in favor of immigration. |
| 2. In the 1800s, immigrants | a unique and complex culture. |
| 3. The Argentinean government | enrich and transform the country. |
| 4. Immigration has created | came from many parts of Europe. |
| 5. New immigrants also | the first immigrants to Argentina. |

**Stop and Think!** What challenges do immigrants experience?

### Glossary

**altitude:** the height of an object or place above sea level

**silver:** a valuable gray metal

**persecution:** violence or discrimination against a group of people

**cuisine:** the food of a specific culture

**enrich:** to add value to something

# Project

**1** **Take the Social Acceptance Survey. Write *All the time, Sometimes* or *Never*.**

**Social Acceptance Survey**

1. Do you feel accepted and valued in your town / community? ____________________
2. Do you make jokes about members of a particular social group? ____________________
3. Can you be yourself around other people? ____________________
4. Do you criticize people for how they look or talk? ____________________
5. Do people treat you differently than they treat other people? ____________________

**2** 41 **Listen and circle for Eva's brother, Josh.**

1. All the time   Sometimes   Never
2. All the time   Sometimes   Never
3. All the time   Sometimes   Never
4. All the time   Sometimes   Never
5. All the time   Sometimes   Never

**3** 42 **Listen and circle for Eva's neighbor, Amber.**

1. All the time   Sometimes   Never
2. All the time   Sometimes   Never
3. All the time   Sometimes   Never
4. All the time   Sometimes   Never
5. All the time   Sometimes   Never



**4** **Look at the survey results on page 121. Circle *T* (True) or *F* (False).**

1. Most people feel accepted and valued in their community.   T   F
2. No one makes jokes about members of other social groups.   T   F
3. A small percentage of people can always be themselves.   T   F
4. A lot of people criticize others sometimes.   T   F
5. No one feels like they are treated differently.   T   F

**5** **Do your own Social Acceptance Survey. Interview people in your community and record your results.**

1. Copy the table in your notebook.
2. Interview five people. Record your results.
3. Form groups and combine your results.
4. Calculate percentages for each answer. Divide by the total number of interviews.
5. Make a report sheet with pie charts for each question.

| | All the Time | Sometimes | Never |
|---|---|---|---|
| 1. Do you feel accepted and valued in your town / community? | 15 | 9 | 1 |
| 2. Do you make jokes about members of a particular social group? | 7 | 12 | 6 |
| 3. Can you be yourself around other people? | 4 | 14 | 7 |
| 4. Do you criticize people for how they look or talk? | 8 | 15 | 2 |
| 5. Do people treat you differently than they treat other people? | 5 | 11 | 9 |

## Social Acceptance Survey

I interviewed five people for the social acceptance survey. Then I combined my results with other group members' results. In total, we surveyed 25 people.

1. Do you feel accepted and valued in your town / community?

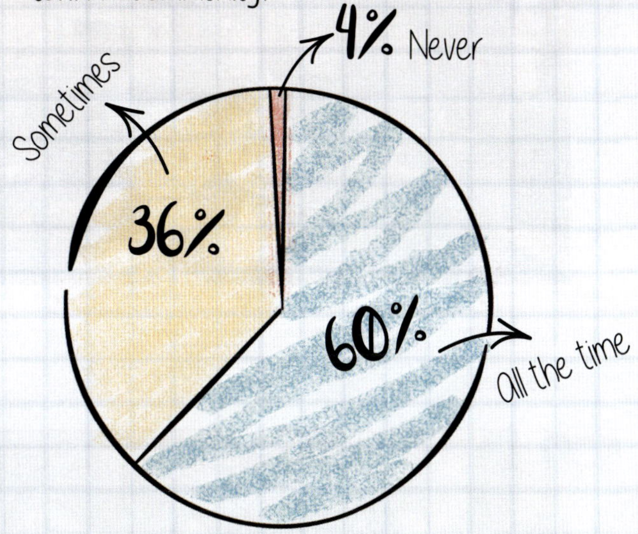


2. Do you make jokes about members of a particular social group?

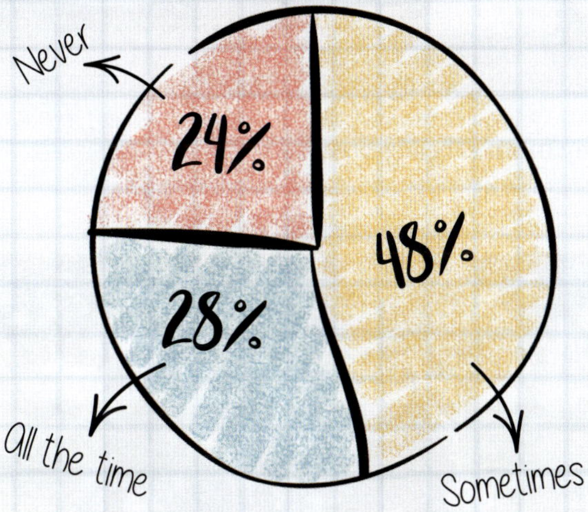


3. Can you be yourself around other people?

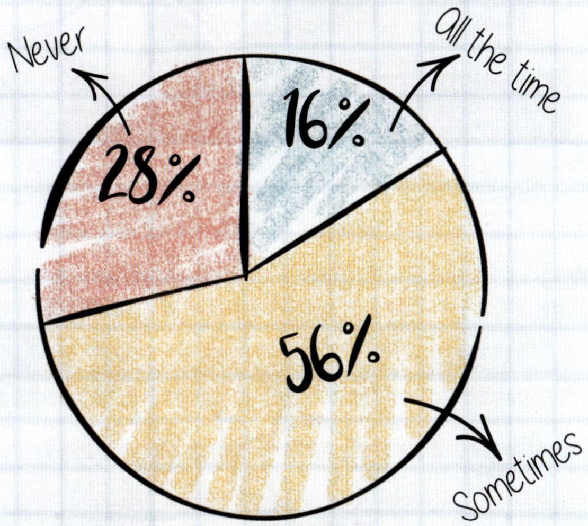


4. Do you criticize people for how they look or talk?

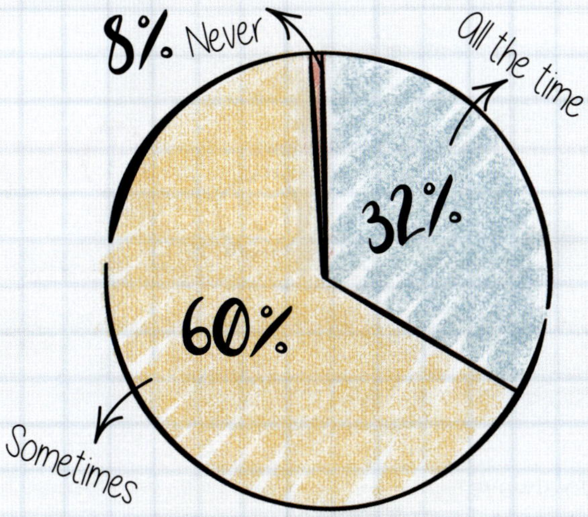


5. Do people treat you differently than they treat other people?

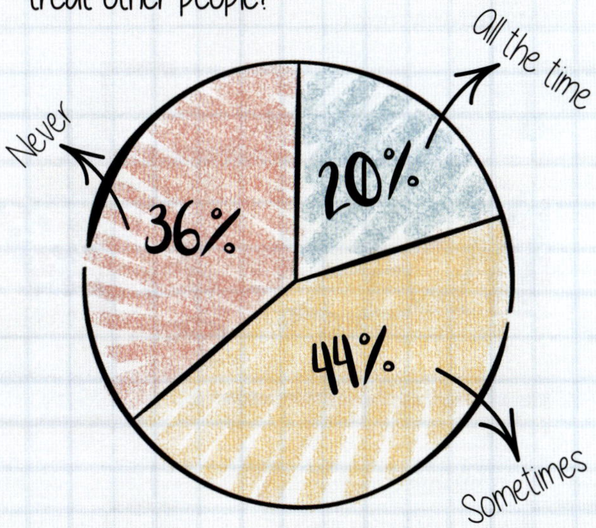

# Review

**1 Look and complete the sentences.**

1

We always ______________________ on the weekend.

5

My brother Owen ______________________ at the gym.

2

I love to ______________________ on my tablet.

6

My mom is really busy so we ______________________ a lot.



3

My sister Maggie ______________________.

7

My friends and I ______________________ at the park after school.

4

My cousins ______________________, but not on school nights.

8

Jo always ______________________ on Saturdays.

## 2 Read and complete using *too* or *either*.

**Tania:** Hi, Matt. I'm watching TV. What are you doing?

**Matt:** I'm watching TV (1) ______________________.

**Tania:** Oh, what are you watching?

**Matt:** It's a nature documentary, actually. I finally don't have any homework to do.

**Tania:** I don't have any homework (2) ______________________. Do you want to see a movie? I haven't seen the new Star Wars movie.

**Matt:** I haven't seen it (3) ______________________. What time does it start?

**Tania:** At five-thirty. I don't need to have dinner, though. I already ate.

**Matt:** Me (4) ______________________. Should we meet there?

**Tania:** That sounds good. See you there!

## 3 Read and match.

| | |
|---|---|
| 1. I love Indian food. | Neither do I. |
| 2. We're going shopping soon. | Neither have I. |
| 3. She can't swim. | So do I. |
| 4. I don't know how to cook. | Neither can I. |
| 5. He's not good at sports. | So are we. |
| 6. I haven't had lunch yet. | Neither am I. |

## 4 Read and answer using *Me too* or *Me neither*.



1
A: I'm going on vacation next week.
B: ______________________.

2
A: I want to go swimming in the ocean.
B: ______________________! And look for seashells.

3
A: I don't like long flights, though.
B: ______________________. But our flight is only two hours.

4
A: I already packed my suitcase!
B: ______________________! I like to be prepared.

5
A: Oh, no! I didn't pack my swimsuit!
B: ______________________. I'm going to buy one there.

6
A: I can't wait!
B: ______________________! I'm so excited!

# Just for Fun

**1 Choose and mark (✓) one option from each set. Then use your selections to complete the silly stories.**

1. a celebration
   - ☐ Thanksgiving
   - ☐ New Year's Eve
   - ☐ Independence Day
2. a celebration activity
   - ☐ set off fireworks
   - ☐ watch a parade
   - ☐ wave flags
3. a symptom or injury
   - ☐ runny nose
   - ☐ sunburn
   - ☐ stomachache
4. an environment action
   - ☐ planting trees
   - ☐ reducing carbon emissions
   - ☐ sending garbage to landfills
5. a fan activity
   - ☐ collect action figures
   - ☐ dress up as a character
   - ☐ get an autograph
6. a keepsake
   - ☐ baby tooth
   - ☐ seashell
   - ☐ toy car
7. a collocation with *get*
   - ☐ get hungry
   - ☐ get thirsty
   - ☐ get lost
8. a habit
   - ☐ go out to eat
   - ☐ work out
   - ☐ order take-out

➤ 124

## Silly Story 1

One day, I was ____________ (AN ENVIRONMENT ACTION) when I started to ____________ (A COLLOCATION WITH GET). I realized that I also had a ____________ (A SYMPTOM OR INJURY). I was alone and I didn't have any money, so I decided to ____________ (A CELEBRATION ACTIVITY) and sell my magic ____________ (A KEEPSAKE). It worked! A man came by. He was on his way to ____________ (A HABIT), so he stopped to ____________ (A CELEBRATION ACTIVITY) with me. He gave me $100 for my magic ____________ (A KEEPSAKE). I used the money to buy lunch and ____________ (A FAN ACTIVITY). It was the best ____________ (A CELEBRATION) ever!

## Silly Story 2

____________ (AN ENVIRONMENT ACTION) on ____________ (A CELEBRATION) isn't easy. First, you need to ____________ (A HABIT). You'll probably get a ____________ (A SYMPTOM OR INJURY) and you might even ____________ (A COLLOCATION WITH GET). Don't worry! Just take out your phone and call a friend to help you ____________ (A CELEBRATION ACTIVITY) with you. Then turn around, clap your hands and show everyone your cousin's shiny yellow ____________ (A KEEPSAKE). Then you'll be able to ____________ (A FAN ACTIVITY) at the supermarket.

# Workbook

1 Unit

## Vocabulary – Celebrations

**1 Look and label.**

a cap
candles
open
and
make
get
a diploma
presents
watch
fireworks
wave
gown
flags
resolutions
set off
a parade
blow out
wear

0a. 
wave flags

0b. 
watch a parade

1a. 
blow out candles

1b. 
open presents

2a. 
get a diploma

2b. 
Wear a cap and gown

3a. 
make resolutions

3b. 
set off fireworks



**2 Look and write the celebration.**

0. Independence Day
1. graduation
2. birthday
3. New year's eve

**3 Read and complete.**

athletes ~~enjoy~~ fireworks
get picnic science watch

Come and (0) enjoy our Annual Sports Day on Saturday, August 27th! At noon, you can (1) watch a parade of (2) athletes. Competitions begin at 1:00 and go until 4 p.m. All athletes will (3) get a certificate for participation. After the competitions, stay for a (4) picnic and watch the (5) science club students set off (6) fireworks.

**Guess What!**
When a person graduates, say *Congratulations!* For many other occasions, we say *Happy* and the name of the event: *Happy Birthday! Happy New Year!*

## Grammar – Present Continuous (future meaning)

**1 Read and match.**

0. We usually use the present continuous — add *-ing* to the end of the verb.
1. We use the verb *be* and — to talk about future plans.
2. We can also use the present continuous — for activities that are happening now.

**2 Read and complete the dialogue.**

coming
meeting
~~doing~~
having
going
~~what~~
~~taking~~

Jamie: Hey, Pete! How are you?

Pete: Fine, thanks. What are you (0) ___doing___ after school?

Jamie: I'm (1) ___taking___ my dog to the vet.

Pete: Oh, is he OK?

Jamie: Yes, he just really needs a bath! (2) ___What___ are you doing tomorrow?

Pete: I'm (3) ___having___ lunch with my family, but I'm free in the afternoon.

Jamie: A couple of friends and I are (4) ___going___ to a fireworks show tomorrow night. Do you want to come?

Pete. That's sounds great. What time are you (5) ___meting___?

Jamie: Around 7 p.m. My sister Lucy is (6) ___coming___, too.

**3 Read and mark (✓).**

| | Now | Future |
|---|---|---|
| 0. Are you coming to my party? | ☐ | ✓ |
| 1. I'm meeting my friends for lunch. | ☒ | ☐ |
| 2. Bruno's busy. He's studying for a test. | ☒ | ☐ |
| 3. It's raining very hard. | ☒ | ☐ |
| 4. Our soccer team is playing on Saturday. | ☐ | ☒ |
| 5. When are you going on vacation? | ☐ | ☒ |

## 4 Complete using the correct forms of the verbs.

0. We ___'re visiting___ (*visit*) my grandparents tomorrow.
1. Julia ___is having___ (*have*) a Halloween party next Friday.
2. We ___are going___ (*go*) to the baseball game tonight!
3. I ___am going___ (*go*) to school tomorrow.
4. Mike and Eva ___are singing___ (*sing*) a song at the school concert.
5. My aunt ___is taking___ (*take*) us to the zoo on Sunday.

## 5 Write the negative forms of the sentences in Activity 4.

0. We aren't visiting my grandparents tomorrow.
1. ______
2. ______
3. ______
4. ______
5. ______

# Review

## 1 Read the clues and guess the celebration activity.

0. to extinguish small fires on a dessert ___blow out candles___
1. to pay attention to people in a procession ___watch a parade___
2. to cause explosions in the sky ___set of fireworks___
3. to have an unusual hat and robe on your body ___wear a cap and grown___
4. to move symbols of a country in the air ___wave flags___

## 2 Unscramble and answer about you.

0. you / doing / right / homework / now / are / ?
   Are you doing homework right now? ___ Yes, I am.
1. going / family / your / today / shopping / is / ?
   ______ ______
2. dentist / the / are / you / to / tomorrow / going / ?
   ______ ______
3. party / having / are / friends / a / this / your / weekend / ?
   ______ ______
4. tomorrow / to / going / are / you / school / ?
   ______ ______

## Reading

### 1 Read and complete the facts.

First half languages Navajo ~~tribes~~

0. There are hundreds of American Indian ___tribes___ in the United States.
1. In Canada, indigenous people prefer the term __________ Nations.
2. About __________ of the states in the US have American Indian names.
3. There are 150 American Indian __________ in the US and Canada.
4. The most common indigenous language is __________.

### 2 Read and complete the mind map in your notebook.

A powwow was once an important **gathering** to negotiate peace between tribes. The name *powwow* comes from a similar-sounding Narragansett word for a healing ceremony. Now the word powwow refers to a type of American Indian gathering that is common in Canada and the United States. At powwows, people of American Indian **heritage** meet to **socialize**, dance, sing and honor their cultures.

A powwow usually starts with a parade of dancers in colorful traditional clothing. The clothing has beautiful designs made with beads and feathers. Then there is singing and dancing to the beat of a drum. Later, there are dancing competitions for men and women. There are also stands where you can buy traditional food, such as grilled corn, **fry bread** and **venison** or **bison**. There are also modern snacks like hot dogs, pizza and lemonade.

Powwows can last for one day, or for up to a week if it is a special occasion. They can be at any time of the year. And they aren't just for American Indians—they're open to everyone. It's a great time to learn about different tribal cultures. There are a few rules you should follow if you go to a powwow: First, it's OK to wear regular clothes to a powwow. Please *don't* dress up like an "Indian." But please *do* wear clothing that is modest and respectful. Many powwows take place during the summer, but no swimsuits please! Lastly, remember to have fun! It's a celebration, after all!



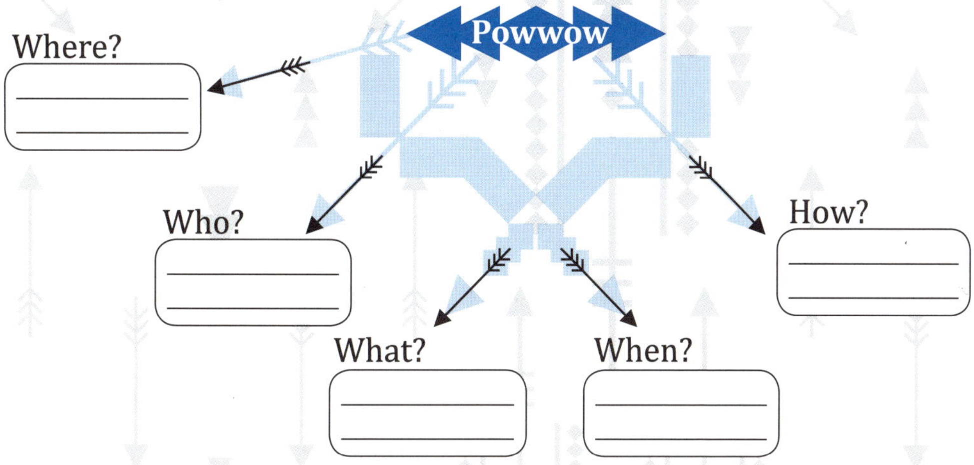


### Glossary

**gathering:** an event with people from different places

**heritage:** ethnicity or culture

**socialize:** to talk to friends

**fry bread:** a flat dough fried in oil

**venison:** meat from deer

**bison:** buffalo meat

# 2 Unit

## Vocabulary – First Aid

**1 Look and complete.**

0. first -aid kit
1. a______ s______
2. i______ p______
3. m______
4. t______
5. b______
6. b______ g______

## Symptoms and Injuries

**2 Look, read and complete.**

bruise cut fever headache runny nose sore throat stomachache sunburn

## Grammar – *Should*

**1 Read and number the suggestions.**

0 My sister has a bad cold. She has a runny nose and a sore throat.

1 My friends and I were at the beach and now we all have a bad sunburn!

2 My dad fell on some ice. Now he has a big bruise on his arm.

3 I got a paper cut. It's very small, but it hurts a lot!

4 I feel very hot and my face is red.

[1] That's not good! You should try to avoid staying in the sun, but now that you have it, burn gel will help it to heal.

[3] You should wash it, use antiseptic spray and put a bandage on it. It will heal in a day or two.

[0] I'm sorry to hear that. She should stay home and drink some hot tea.

[2] Ouch! He should put an ice pack on it. It should get better soon.

[4] Oh, you have a fever. You should check your temperature and then take some medicine.

### Short Answers

**Should** I go to the doctor?

Yes, you **should**.

No, you **shouldn't**.

**2 Complete the sentences using *should* or *shouldn't*.**

0. You should eat vegetables every day.
1. You shouldn't skip breakfast.
2. You should always wear a seatbelt.
3. You should avoid foods with a lot of sugar.
4. You shouldn't stay in the sun too long.

**3 Unscramble and answer.**

0. I / to / should / at / bed / midnight / go
   Should I go to bed at midnight? No, you shouldn't.
1. for / junk food / should / eat / I / lunch
   Should i eat junk food for? lunch No, you shouldn't
2. I / my / wash / should / hands / before / dinner
   Should i wash my hand before diner yes, you should
3. should / brush / teeth / I / my / night / at
   Should i brush my teeth at night yes, you should

# 2 Unit

## Zero Conditional

**4 Read and underline the condition.**

0. When you lift weights, you make your muscles stronger.
1. When kids eat a lot of junk food, they don't get enough nutrients.
2. People have trouble concentrating if they don't sleep well.
3. If I exercise regularly, I feel great.
4. Students feel more prepared when they study every night.

**5 Read and match.**

| | |
|---|---|
| 0. Life is less stressful if | you make your heart stronger. |
| 1. You lose weight if | you have routines. |
| 2. Your relationships suffer | your body doesn't function well. |
| 3. When you exercise, | your body gets the right nutrients. |
| 4. If you don't exercise, | when you spend too much time online. |
| 5. You protect your teeth | you eat fewer calories. |
| 6. When you eat a balanced diet, | when you brush them. |

**Zero Conditionals**

We can also use negative forms in zero conditional sentences:

If you **don't** eat fruits and vegetables, your body **doesn't** get important nutrients.



## Review

**1 Read and correct the sentences.**

0. You should ~~to eat~~ a balanced diet.
   You should eat a balanced diet.
1. If you have a cold, your body need rest.
   ______________________
2. People shouldn't going to school when they are sick.
   ______________________
3. When you wash your hands you wash off viruses and bacteria.
   ______________________
4. If people see ads for junk food, they wanted to buy it.
   ______________________

# Animals Who Help

## Reading

**1 Look and read. What is happening in the picture?**

- [ ] The boy's pet is visiting him at the hospital.
- [x] The dog has a job. It visits hospital **patients**.
- [ ] Doctors are treating the dog at the hospital.

**2 Read and answer *T* (True) or *F* (False).**

Animals and humans share a special connection. Animals make loyal companions, and some even work for humans. More and more, animals are participating in medical treatment to help patients. The use of these animals can improve a patient's physical, social and **cognitive** wellness. Therapy animals and service animals are two animal occupations where animals help humans to be healthy.

Therapy animals often visit hospitals or **nursing homes**. Patients receive many benefits: less pain and less fear—especially for children receiving medical treatment. Therapy animals can help patients to recover from severe injuries, manage **grief** after a traumatic event or find personal strength to overcome anxiety. Therapy animals help people to relax, smile, even laugh. Interacting with a therapy animal can even reduce a person's blood pressure. And animal therapy isn't just for dogs. There are also therapy horses, cats, birds and even fish. Many are pets with special training. They work with their owners to visit and encourage people.

Service animals are like therapy animals, except instead of visiting people, they live with patients. They are usually dogs, and they help people with a range of health conditions ranging from blindness to epilepsy. Some service dogs can guide a blind person through a busy neighborhood. Others can identify when a dangerous medical problem is about to occur or help a child with a physical disability to walk. Some service dogs help people with autism to **cope with** difficult situations. Service animals need a lot of training, and that training is specific to the need of their future owner. Because service animals are so important to the health and **well-being** of their humans, they can go anywhere: to stores, on planes—any place their person needs to go.

0. Therapy animals and service animals help humans to feel well. (T) F
1. Many different types of animals can be therapy animals. (T) F
2. Therapy animals only work in hospitals. T (F)
3. Service animals are pets that visit hospitals and nursing homes. T (F)
4. Service animals are usually dogs. (T) F
5. They are useful for different kinds of health conditions. (T) F
6. Service dogs can't go everywhere with their owners. T (F)

**3 Complete the chart.**

Therapy Animals

Service Animals



### Glossary

**patients:** people who receive medical treatment

**cognitive:** related to the brain

**nursing homes:** places for people who need regular medical care

**grief:** sadness and loss, often after a death

**cope with:** to live and be well in spite of circumstances

**well-being:** health and happiness

## Vocabulary – The Environment

### 1 Look and complete the sentences.

conserve planting ~~polluting~~ reducing saves send use (x2)

It's ___polluting___ the environment.

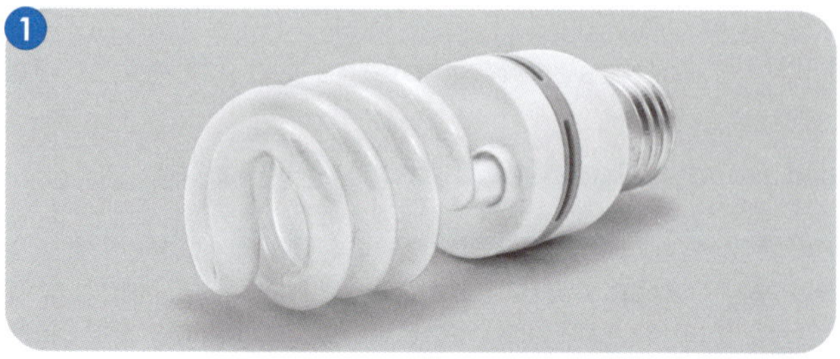

It ______ electricity.

They're ______ trees.

They ______ clean energy.

They ______ fossil fuels.

We ______ a lot of garbage to landfills.

Collecting rainwater is one way to ______ water.

______ carbon emissions is important for the environment.

### 2 Correct the spelling errors.

0. fossil feuls ___fossil fuels___
1. elctricity ______
2. clean enerjy ______
3. garbidge ______
4. landfils ______
5. polution ______
6. envirenment ______

## Grammar – First Conditional

**1 Read and underline the consequence.**

0. If people pick up after their dogs, the city will be much cleaner____________.
1. If people conserve water now, we will have enough water in the future.
2. We will pollute the environment more if we use a lot of electricity.
3. If we play loud music, we will bother our neighbors.
4. We will make our cities nicer if we plant more trees.
5. If we recycle, we will send less garbage to landfills.

**2 Complete using the correct form of the verb.**

0. If people don't pick up after their dogs, the city ____will be____ (*be*) very dirty.
1. If you ____________ (*listen*) to very loud music, you will damage your ears.
2. If we don't control light pollution, we ____________ (*not be able*) to see the stars.
3. If you take long showers, you ____________ (*use*) a lot of water.
4. If we ____________ (*share*) our cars, we will reduce our carbon footprint.
5. If we all work together, we ____________ (*make*) a difference.

**3 Read and switch the order of the condition and the consequence.**

0. If we use regular lightbulbs, we will use more electricity.
   We will use more electricity if we use regular lightbulbs.
1. If we use cold water to wash clothes, we will save electricity.
   ________________________
2. If we don't use clean energy, we will change the Earth's climate.
   ________________________
3. Many animals will go extinct if the Earth's climate changes.
   ________________________

**4 Look and write the questions. Then answer.**

0. what / people / do ... if / sea levels / rise / ?
   What will people do if sea levels rise?
   ________________________
1. where / people / live ... if / cities / disappear underwater / ?
   ________________________
   ________________________
2. what / happen ... if / many animals / go extinct / ?
   ________________________
   ________________________
3. how / we / grow food ... if / bees / go extinct / ?
   ________________________
   ________________________

# 3 Unit

## Review

### 1 Read and correct the sentences.

0. If we will use clean energy, we reduce our carbon footprint.
   *If we use clean energy, we will reduce our carbon footprint.*
1. If people doesn't conserve water, there won't be enough water in the future.
   ______
2. If there isn't enough water we won't be able to grow food.
   ______
3. We will change the climate if we doesn't reduce carbon emissions.
   ______

### 2 Answer about you.

1. Which activity is most important for your city or neighborhood? Why?
   planting trees    conserving water    picking up trash    recycling
   ______
2. List two things that you do to save electricity.
   ______
   ______
3. List two things that you do to conserve water.
   ______
   ______

### 3 Read the actions and write the impact they have on the environment.

0. I wear a sweater in the house when it is cold. — *You're saving electricity on heating.*
1. We use an electric car. — ______
2. We take our paper to a recycling center. — ______
3. I water my plants with a **bucket**, not a **hose.** — ______

### 4 Write two more similar exchanges.

1. ______ — ______
2. ______ — ______

**Glossary**

**bucket:** an open container with a handle used to carry water

**hose:** a flexible tube used to water plants, put out fires, etc.

## Reading

**1 Read quickly and answer. What requires the most water?**

a) our food  b) home use  c) factory products

# YOUR WATER FOOTPRINT

Every day, human beings use an enormous amount of water. On average, a person uses 130 liters of water at home to take a shower, **flush** the toilet, wash clothing and cook. We only drink a small amount, less than two liters. We use much more water—167 liters a day—in factories to make products such as paper, cotton and clothing. But the real surprise is that we use 3,496 liters of water for our food.

Why do we use so much water for food? Let's look at one example. To produce beef for hamburgers, we must provide food and water to a cow for three years. Just the food for the cow requires 3 million liters of water to grow. During its lifetime, the cow also drinks 24,000 liters of water. At the end of the process, for one kilo of beef, we use 15,400 liters of water—enough to fill a wall of water bottles 8 meters high and 40 meters wide.

What can we do about this situation? First of all, we can eat less meat, and when we *do* eat meat, we should choose meat from smaller animals like chickens. And remember other sources of protein like fish, eggs and soy. Second, we should drink less milk and eat less cheese. It is healthier to get nutrients from nuts and vegetables, and it uses less water. Finally, we can reduce food waste. In some countries, people throw away 30% of the food. Be sure to shop at farmer's markets and supermarkets that don't waste food just because it has imperfections—food that is good to eat, but has an unusual shape or color. Remember to wash and dry fresh fruits and vegetables and keep them in a cool, dry place. Use them before they **go bad**. And don't buy it if you aren't going to eat it.

Water is a vital resource, and one that we should protect. Reduce your water footprint today!

**2 Read and underline the information. Write the amount.**

0. the amount of water we use at home  130 liters
1. the amount of water we drink  ______
2. the amount of water in factory products  ______
3. the amount of water to produce food  ______
4. the amount of water to produce 1 kg of beef  ______
5. the percent of food people throw away  ______

137

**3 Decode the water footprint for each item (1=a, 2=b, etc.).**

0 c,ahb

cheese 3,182 liters / kilo

1 a,ghf

sugar ______ liters / kilo

2 hbb

apples ______ liters / kilo

3 ah,hhe

coffee ______ liters / kilo

# 4 Unit

## Vocabulary – Fan Activities

**1 Look and complete the phrases.**

0.  put ___on___ face paint
1.  wear a ____________
2.  ____________ in line
3.  put ____________ posters
4.  be good ____________
5.  dress up ____________ characters
6.  ____________ an autograph
7.  collect action ____________
8.  wear ____________ colors
9.  be a ____________ of

**2 Read and number.**

0. We love jazz music. We listen to it all the time.
1. I waited for hours. There were a lot of people. Finally, I got a ticket to the concert.
2. My brother loves rock music. He has giant pictures of rock bands in his room.
3. Tomorrow is the big game. Remember your red and yellow T-shirts!
4. A famous athlete wrote his signature on my jersey.
5. She has a baseball cap for her favorite team. It's on her head.
6. We want to show that we are big fans, so we put bright colors on our faces.
7. She has more than one hundred superhero characters.
8. Some people think we're strange, but we love wearing costumes!
9. My brother can change his voice to talk like famous actors.

___0___ We're fans of jazz music.

_____ She collects action figures.

_____ I got his autograph!

_____ She's wearing a hat.

_____ We put on face paint.

_____ I stood in line.

_____ He's good at imitating actors' voices.

_____ We dress up as characters.

_____ Wear team colors.

_____ He puts up posters.

## Grammar – Intensifiers

**1 Number the intensifiers from least (0) to most intense (3).**

_______ so/really _______ pretty _______ extremely ___0___ a bit

### Intensifiers

Intensifiers are words that modify adjectives and adverbs:

The athlete is **extremely** fast.

She runs **pretty** fast.

**2 Complete the dialogue using intensifiers.**

**MIKE:** Hi, Gianna. Did you go to the Sci-Fi Festival yet?

**GIANNA:** No. I'm going this afternoon. How is it?

**MIKE:** It's (0) ___really___ (!!!) cool. They have movies there, too. I watched *Planet of the Apes.* I didn't know sci-fi movies were (1) __________ (!!) entertaining. It was (2) __________ (!) long, though.

**GIANNA:** What else do they have at the festival?

**MIKE:** Well, the snacks and drinks are (3) __________ (!!) good. They have pepperoni pizza and chocolate chip cookies!

**GIANNA:** Did they have the costume contest yet?

**MIKE:** No, it's this afternoon.

**GIANNA:** Oh, good!

**MIKE:** You should see the fan art exhibition, too. Some of the artists are amazing! Their posters are (4) __________ (!!!!) realistic.

**GIANNA:** Cool! I can't wait!

## Already, Yet

**3 Look and circle the correct option.**

0 

1 

2 

0. Did they buy any snacks yet?
   (Yes, they did.) / No, they didn't.
1. Did they get into the festival yet?
   Yes, they did. / No, they didn't.
2. Did they already put on their costumes?
   Yes, they did. / No, they didn't.

### Guess What!

It is also possible to use *already* in questions when we expect an affirmative answer: Did you **already** have lunch?

**4 Read and circle T (True) or F (False).**

0. We usually use *already* and *yet* to talk about the past. (T) F
1. We use *already* and *yet* with *Wh-* questions. T F
2. We use *already* and *yet* with *Yes-No* questions. T F
3. *Already* usually goes after the main verb in a sentence. T F
4. *Yet* always goes at the end of a sentence or question. T F

**5 Unscramble and write.**

0. get / you / yet / any / did / autographs / ?
   Did you get any autographs yet?
1. a / watch / did / yet / you / movie / ?
   ____________________
2. to / we / art / already / exhibition / went / the / .
   ____________________
3. already / registered / the / she / for / contest / .
   ____________________
4. have / did / already / you / some / snacks / ?
   ____________________

## Review

**1 Read and correct the sentences.**

0. I'm a fan ~~for space movies.~~
   I'm a fan of space movies.
1. My friends and I dress up of characters.
   ____________________
2. My sister put on posters in her room.
   ____________________
3. For big games, we put up face paint.
   ____________________
4. Ryan is really good in dancing.
   ____________________
5. I stood at line for three hours.
   ____________________



**2 Read and complete the sentences.**

0. Sara ___already___ gave her presentation.
1. Max didn't see the art exhibition ____________.
2. Did you make your costume ____________?
3. Did you ____________ have some snacks and drinks?
4. Lisa didn't see the movie ____________.

## Reading

**1 Read and mark (✓) the topics in the article. Then circle the main idea of the article.**

☐ famous players ☑ the number of fans ☐ the history of the club ☐ team colors ☐ rival teams

☐ sponsors ☐ the cost for fans ☐ video games ☐ how to watch a game

# Real Madrid: The World's Most Valuable Sports Team

The world's most valuable sports team is Real Madrid, a famous soccer club. The club dates to 1902, when soccer first became popular in Spain. Now, more than a **century** later, the team is worth $3.26 billion dollars. This is more than any other sports team in the world!

One reason the club is worth so much is because fans buy Real Madrid jerseys and other **merchandise**. And there are a lot of fans—450 million fans worldwide! There are fan clubs from Boston to Jakarta. Real Madrid also makes a lot of money from TV channels that broadcast their games. In addition, they receive money from **sponsors**. Real Madrid's sponsors include Audi, Adidas, Coca-Cola, Emirates Airlines and Microsoft. Adidas alone pays $800 million dollars a year in sponsorship.

Being a Real Madrid fan can be expensive. Tickets to a **home game** at Santiago Bernabéu Stadium in Madrid cost a minimum of $35 per person, but can be $250 or more. Many fans buy scarves, jerseys and hats with the team colors, white and gray. Some **devoted** fans go to **away games** in other cities in Spain or even other countries. Fans pay for the tickets and for travel expenses: airfare, hotels and taxis.

Of course you don't have to spend a fortune to be a *Madridista*—the name for a Real Madrid fan. You can always follow the team in the news or watch on TV. You can also pay to watch individual games online for about $10.



**2 Read and match.**

| | |
|---|---|
| 0. the value of the team | current team colors |
| 1. Jakarta | $3.26 billion dollars |
| 2. Microsoft | a sponsor |
| 3. white and gray | $10 |
| 4. Santiago Bernabéu | the name of a stadium |
| 5. the minimum cost of a ticket | $35 |
| 6. the cost to watch a game online | the location of one fan club |

### Glossary

**century:** 100 years

**merchandise:** things that a company sells

**sponsors:** companies that give money to support an athlete, team or organization

**home game:** a game in a team's home stadium

**devoted:** dedicated; loyal

**away game:** a game in another team's stadium

## 5 Unit

## Vocabulary – Personal Experiences

**1 Look, read and number.**

0

1

2

3

4

5

- You made a mistake. The result is 564, not 543. [ ]
- I bought a lot of souvenirs there. [ ]
- Oh, no! I forgot it was his birthday! [0]
- Stay on the trail. You don't want to get lost in the forest. [ ]
- I saw it in the park and immediately fell in love with it. [ ]
- I think I am going to get in trouble... [ ]

### Keepsakes

**2 Find and circle names of five keepsakes.**

bjnecklaceksbabytoothdfrdrawingsowseashellfidtoycartdk

**Guess What!**
The words *foot*, *tooth* have irregular plural form: one tooth, two teeth; one foot, two feet



**3 Complete the sentences using the words from Activity 2.**

0. Emma Watson wore a long black dress and a diamond ___necklace___ to the award ceremony.
1. My mom has a jar full of ______________. Mine, my sister's and my brother's. They are old and pretty ugly.
2. The ______________ I made in preschool is still hanging on our refrigerator.
3. I love holding this ______________ to my ear to hear the ocean.
4. My grandma still has that old ______________ in the closet. She says I loved playing with it.

## Grammar – Past Continuous

**1 Look and answer the questions.**

Yesterday at 10:10 a.m...

0. Was Alan paying attention?

   *No, he wasn't.*

1. Were Gina and Hal giving a presentation?

   ______________________________

2. Was Miss Smith reading a book?

   ______________________________

3. Were Claire, Emma and Pam sleeping?

   ______________________________

4. Was Bill reading?

   ______________________________

### Short Answers

**Was** he drink**ing**?
Yes, he **was**. / No, he **wasn't**.

**Were** they eat**ing**?
Yes, they **were**. / No, they **weren't**.

### Past Continuous: *While*

**2 Look again and write sentences using *while*.**

Yesterday at 10:10 a.m...

0. Gina and Hal / Miss Smith

   *Gina and Hal were giving a presentation while Miss Smith was writing.*

1. Alan / Bill

   ______________________________

2. Miss Smith / Claire, Emma and Pam

   ______________________________

3. Bill / Gina and Hal

   ______________________________

# 5 Unit

## Past Continuous and Past Simple: *When*

**3 Write sentences using *when*.**

0

do yoga

2

ride his bike

1

walk her dog

3

study for a math exam

0. earthquake start
   She was doing yoga when the earthquake started.
1. see an accident
   ______________________________
2. his telephone ring
   ______________________________
3. someone knock at the door
   ______________________________



## Review

**1 Complete the table.**

| | Present Simple | Past Simple | Past Continuous |
|---|---|---|---|
| he | make a mistake | made a mistake | was making a mistake |
| they | get in trouble | | |
| I | | prepared breakfast | |
| she | | | was drinking |
| computer | works | | |
| Dad | | bought souvenirs | |
| they | have a lot of fun | | |

## Reading

**1** Read and underline two **hormones** that affect your body clock.

**2** Read again and mark the times for each activity on the timeline.

0. thinking creatively 1. having a light meal 2. sleeping
3. doing exercise 4. having a short sleep

| 0 | | | | |
|---|---|---|---|---|
| 9:00 a.m. | 3:00 p.m. | 6:00 p.m. | 8:00 p.m. | 10:00 p.m. |
| noon | 4:00 p.m. | 8:00 p.m. | 10:00 p.m. | 6:00 a.m. |

Ring, ring! The alarm goes off. How are you feeling? Fresh and ready to go, or tired and **sluggish**? Believe it or not, there is a scientific explanation for this. Your body has an internal clock that marks the ideal times for your activities and rest. Let's check it out!

# Your Body Clock

The moment you wake up, the production of the sleep hormone, melatonin, stops. The best time to do it is around 6 a.m. To feel fully awake, go out to direct light as soon as you wake up. If you have a dog, walk it—you will feel awake immediately. Between 9:00 a.m. and noon, your mind is at its maximum level of alertness. At this time of the day, the stress hormone, cortisol, keeps your brain active. It's a good time to be creative. And to have a math class!

The best time to have a big meal of the day is around 3 p.m. Is this when you finish school? If so, you must feel very hungry. Eat and let your body **digest** the food. And maybe take a short nap!

From 6:00 to 8:00 p.m. your body temperature increases, your **heart** and **lungs** work better and your muscles are 6% stronger than at other times of the day. As a result, this is a great time to do exercise. Go to the gym, run around the park or simply jump rope! Any exercise is fine as long as you do it regularly.

In the evening, the brain produces melatonin to make you sleepy. Don't eat heavy meals after 8 p.m. Your digestion is much slower in the evening and you can easily gain weight. Don't look at bright screens on tablets or phones because the light can change your body chemistry and make it hard to fall asleep. As the melatonin takes effect, your body temperature goes down and you'll feel like going to bed. From 10 p.m. to 6:00 a.m., the brain is cleaning out the waste **toxins** from a hard day of thinking.

So, is this what your day is like?

3 min **3 Think Fast!** In your notebook, draw a timeline about your day.



### Glossary

**hormone:** natural substance that controls activities in the body

**sluggish:** not alert, slow in movement

**digest:** process food in the stomach

**heart:** 

**lungs:** 

**toxins:** poisonous substances that cause disease

6 Unit

# Vocabulary – Travel

**1 Unscramble and match. Then look and number the photos.**

0. hxeangce ___exchange___ — money
1. irhe ______________
2. yast ______________
3. okob ______________
4. chatc ______________
5. teg ______________
6. capk ______________

a guide
a suitcase
in a hotel
a flight
a passport
a train
money

0

## Collocations

146 **2 Read and complete the sentences.**

0. My sister gets ___angry___ when I ask her to wash the dishes.
1. I get very ______________ when I exercise, so I always carry a bottle of water.
2. My brother always gets ______________ late—and he sets three alarms!
3. My sister is on a diet, but it's difficult because she gets ______________ very quickly.
4. I have to get ______________ for the math exam next week.
5. I look forward to my vacation in Hawaii. When I get ______________, I'm going straight to the beach.
6. My aunt gets ______________ every time she visits the city. I'm going to buy her a GPS.
7. If I'm going to finish this homework, I need to get ______________ soon.

## Grammar – Present Perfect

1 **Read and complete using *ever* and the present perfect.**

### Short Answers

When you ask about life experiences using *ever*, you use the present perfect. When you want to specify the exact moment you did something, you use the past simple:

**Has** he **been** to South Africa?

No, he **hasn't**.

**Have** you ever **eaten** curry?

Yes, I **have**. I **ate** curry in India.

0. (*be*) Have you ever been to China?
   Yes, I have. I went to China in 2015.
1. (*try chai tea*) ____________________
   Yes, he has. He tried chai tea in India.
2. (*get lost*) ____________________
   Yes, she has. She got lost in the mountains last summer.
3. (*take a train*) ____________________
   Yes, they have. They took a train in Europe.
4. (*live abroad*) ____________________
   Yes, I have. I lived in Italy for a year.

### Guess What!

In American English, the past participle of got is gotten: *Has she ever gotten lost?* Other past participle forms are the same as the past simple forms: *tried, traveled, lived, had.*

2 **Look and write sentences using *already* and *yet*.**

0. I have already seen a family of elephants.
1. ____________________
2. ____________________
3. ____________________
4. ____________________
5. ____________________
6. ____________________

Things to do:

see a family of elephants ✓
take pictures ✓
watch a sunset ✓
eat bobotie ✗
give monkey bananas ✗
buy souvenirs ✗
hear a lion roar ✓

## 6 Unit

**3 Read and circle the correct option.**

0. Have you **been** / **gone** to the supermarket? Yes, I I bought some chocolates.
1. Have you **been** / **gone** to the new mall? No, not yet.
2. Has he **been** / **gone** to France? Yes, he's enjoying every moment of his trip!
3. Have they **been** / **gone** on vacation? Yes, they're staying at a hotel near the beach.
4. Has she **been** / **gone** to the movies? Yes, she loved the movie.

### Been, Gone

We can use *been* and *gone* to talk about visiting a place, but there is a difference in meaning:
Have you **been** to New Zealand? Yes, I have. (This means you are not there now.)
Has he **gone** to London? Yes, he has. (This means he is there now.)

## Review

**1 Read and complete the e-mail.**

hot hungry lost ready started ~~there~~ thirsty up

mail.google.com

**From:** marktraveller@gmail.com
**To:** dadatwork@gmail.com
**Subject:** mexico

Hi, Dad! We finally went to see the pyramids of Teotihuacan. We had a lot of fun, but we almost didn't get ___there___. First, we got ______ late because our alarm clocks didn't go off. Then it took a long time for us to get ______ because I couldn't find my sunglasses. Finally, we got ______ on our trip. But we didn't get very far. We got ______ looking for the bus station. We found it, but we got ______ waiting for the bus. We forgot to take snacks! And by the time we got to the pyramids, the weather was getting ______. We got very ______ climbing up all of the steps of the pyramids! Fortunately, we were able to buy some water there. Later, we went to a nearby town to have lunch. We had some delicious tacos! It was a difficult day, but we had a great time! I'll send you some photos later!

Love,

Mark

## Reading

**1 Look at the map and circle the correct option.**

0. It's a map of **Saudi Arabia** / **India**.
1. Kanyakumari and Dibrugarh are small **islands** / **cities**.
2. The line represents a **railway** / **river**.
3. The article is probably about **shopping** / **transportation**.

**2 Read the article and match the numbers with their meaning.**

# The Longest Train

### Have you ever been on a train? An easy question? Well, let me rephrase it...

Have you ever spent more than 80 hours on the same train? No? Maybe it is time for an adventure, then!

Railways in India date back to 1848, when British colonists realized there was a great need to connect the different parts of this huge country. Now the railway system has grown so much that India has one of the biggest railway networks in the world—just enough to provide service for India's 1.2 billion people!

Selling snacks

So, let's board the Dibrugarh-Kanyakumari Vivek Express! Indian Railway number 15906 is the longest train line in India, both in terms of travel time and distance. During your trip, you will cover a distance of 4,281 km in 3 days, 11 hours and 5 minutes. Yes, that's right! You will leave on a Saturday night from Dibrugarh station in the northeastern state of Assam, the land of tea-growers, and you will arrive in Kanyakumari, in the buzzing business-oriented state of Tamil Nadu on Wednesday morning. You will be traveling on a 21-car train in company of 1,800 other passengers!

Admiring the view

You should also know that there are different classes of cars on your train. If you are a poor student, you can't afford the air-conditioned cars with beds, which cost around $60 per person. You can get a ticket on a sleeper car without air conditioning, but if you really want to save money, or you can't book your ticket in advance, you have only one option: unreserved. There are no beds—just wooden benches if you are the first one to arrive. If you arrive late, you can sit on the floor or hang in a hammock. It's the perfect solution for a poor student at only $9.

Now that you're on the train, what can you do during your three-and-a-half-day trip? Take photographs, read—or simply shop! You will see a lot of people at railway stations selling everything you can imagine: candy and peanuts, fingernail scissors and pens, samosas and bananas—but most of all *chai*, tea with milk, sugar and sometimes spices. You can have hundreds of tiny cups of chai in all the hours to come!

Samosas and chai

Enjoy your trip! India's beauty will amaze you.

_____ number of passengers

_____ the population of India

_____ the distance of the trip

_____ the price of a ticket in an air-conditioned car with a bed

__0__ the beginning of construction of railways in India

_____ the railway number

_____ the number of train cars

# 7 Unit

## Vocabulary – Extreme Sports

**1 Read and match to form extreme sports.**

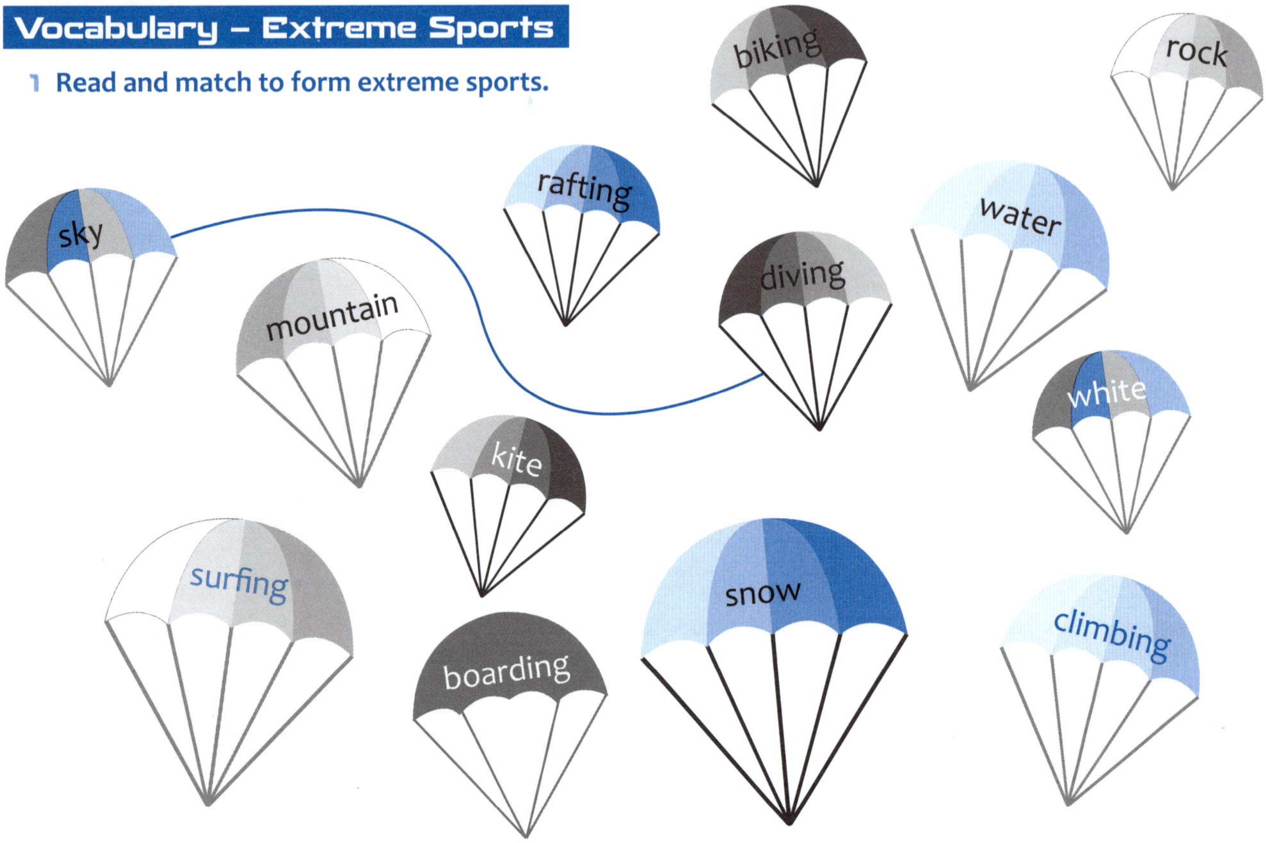


**2 Read the descriptions and write the name of the extreme sport.**

0 It was fascinating. I was flying like a bird!

skydiving

1 We rode on a trail in the forest for 15 kilometers. It was exhausting!

________________

2 It was freezing, but the view from the mountain was breathtaking.

________________

3 The place isn't far away, and it's a good place to practice before we try higher mountains.

________________

4 The water was wild! The raft turned over twice, but we had fun.

________________

5 It was a good lesson. I managed to keep the kite in the air for a long time. My instructor was very helpful.

________________

150

## Adjectives

**3 Circle the correct option.**

0. I am **terrified / terrifying** of heights.
1. The experience of hiking in the mountains was **thrilled / thrilling**.
2. The radio presenter was so **bored / boring** that I fell asleep.
3. I was **tired / tiring** after the bike ride.
4. The rollercoaster wasn't as **excited / exciting** as I hoped.
5. She was very **interested / interesting** in his speech.

## Grammar – *Might*

1 Look and write sentences using *might.*

0. (*take / compass*) I might take a compass.
1. (*take photos*) ______
2. (*run / 10 km*) ______
3. (*visit / Butterfly Sanctuary*) ______
4. (*get thirsty*) ______
5. (*wear / life jacket*) ______

**Guess What!**
We use *would* for hypothetical situations in the future.

## *Would*

2 Unscramble the sentences. Then look and number the situations.

0. never / would / him / I / party / invite / to / a I would never invite him to a party.
1. in / Would / train / by / Europe / you / travel ______
2. live / Canada / We / in / would / never ______
3. jungle adventure / a / she / ever / go / Would / trip / on ______
4. go / would / She / skydiving / never ______

# 7 Unit

## Present Perfect: *Never*

**3 Look and complete using the present perfect and *never*.**

0

Have you ever baked a birthday cake?

No, I haven't.

I 've never baked a birthday cake.

1

Have you ever gone diving in the Indian Ocean?

No, I ______________.

I ______________________________ in the Indian Ocean.

2

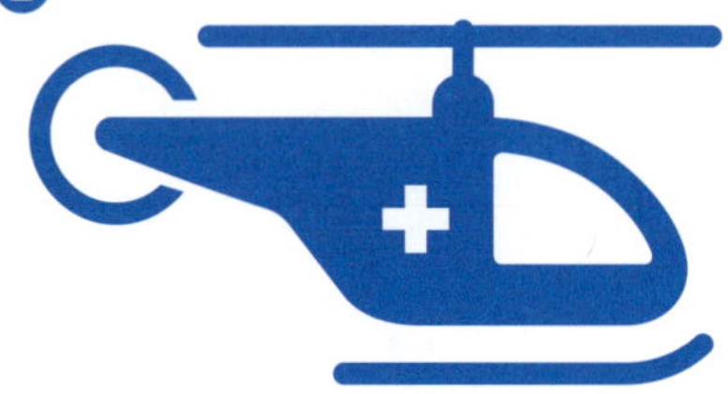

Have they ever flown in a helicopter?

No, they ______________.

They ______________________________ in a helicopter.

3

Has she ever sung karaoke?

No, she ______________.

She ______________________________ karaoke.

4

Has he ever gone skydiving?

No, he ______________.

He ______________________________ skydiving.

5

Have they ever been to France?

No, they ______________.

They ______________________________ to France.

152 **Review**

**1 Read and complete the sentences using participle adjectives.**

0. This is a boring movie. I am bored.
1. She is interested in the topic. The topic is ______________________________.
2. The adventure was thrilling. All the participants felt ______________________________.
3. The news was ______________________________. Everybody was excited.
4. I felt tired. The trip to the forest was really ______________________________.
5. The encounter with the bear was terrifying. We were ______________________________.

## Reading

**1 Read the article and underline the adjectives that don't describe Bethany.**

boring · determined · inspiring · lucky · brave · disabled · unprofessional · terrifying

**2 Read again and underline the following information.**

0. Bethany's last name
1. the day of the accident
2. the name of her friend
3. the title of the movie
4. her latest competition
5. meaning of "wildcard"

soulsurfer.com

ABOUT CONNECT WITH GOD GALLERY

# *Soul Surfer*

Bethany Hamilton was born in Hawaii on February 8, 1990. Both her parents were surfers, so she was introduced to surfing at a very young age. She began competing at the age of eight and at 11 she won the Haleiwa Menehune competition in two categories. After the competition, she was offered a **sponsorship** and she started to **pursue** her professional **career**.

October 31, 2003 was just like any other morning for Bethany. She woke up early, and by 7:30 a.m. she was already on the beach with her surfboard. She was with her friend Alana, Alana's father and Alana's brother. The ocean was calm, so they got into the water to paddle on their boards, waiting for the waves to **pick up**. Bethany was lying on her surfboard with her arms in water when suddenly she felt a tremendous pressure on her left arm. At first, she didn't feel any pain, but she was terrified when she saw the water near her turn red. In a matter of seconds, her friends realized that a tiger shark had attacked Bethany. Her left arm was gone. Alana's father quickly made a **tourniquet** using his surfboard leash, got everyone out of the water and got Bethany to the hospital. In spite of losing 60% of her blood, Bethany survived.

Bethany was back in the water only a month after the shark attack. Her amazing recovery was a result of passion, determination and **faith**. Later, she won several competitions—proving that a loss of arm was not an obstacle to fulfilling her surfing goals. Inspired by her story, the movie *Soul Surfer* was released in 2011.

Bethany Hamilton appeared in the news again in 2016 when she participated in and won third place in a World Surf League's Fiji Woman's Pro competition. She entered as a wildcard, which means she wasn't considered a top surfer. She is a great example of an athlete whose passion cannot be stopped by any adversity. Nowadays, Bethany is still living in Hawaii with her husband and her son, Tobias.

### Glossary

**soul:** a spiritual part of a person

**sponsorship:** money an organization pays someone in exchange for the right to advertise

**pursue:** to try to get or do something over a period of time

**career:** a job of profession

**pick up:** to gradually increase

**tourniquet:** a bandage, strip of cloth, etc., that is tied around an injured body part to slow the bleeding

**faith:** strong belief

# 8 Unit

## Vocabulary – Habits

**1 Decode the names of habits. Then number the photos.**

0. work out
1. ____ _ _______
2. __ ___ __ ___
3. ____ ___
4. _____ ____-___
5. _____ __
6. ____ __ ____
7. ______ ______

## Grammar – Too, Either

**1 Unscramble and write.**

0. hate / papaya / I

   I hate papaya.

   I do too.

1. she / sleeps in / often

   ______________________

   (he) ______________________

2. every day / work out / don't / I

   ______________________

   (she) ______________________

3. can't / today / with / she / hang out / them

   ______________________

   (I) ______________________

4. is / our / cool / teacher / English

   ______________________

   (math teacher) ______________________

5. with / happy / aren't / results / they / the football

   ______________________

   (we) ______________________

## So, Neither

**2 Read and number the lines of the dialogue.**

**Tom:** So did I. What did you think? ☐

**Natalia:** Yes, I did. I streamed it live on my computer. ☐

**Natalia:** I don't want to talk about it either! ☐

**Natalia:** It was horrible. I thought they were going to win. ☐

**Tom:** Did you see the game last night? 0

**Tom:** So did I. Then, at the last second, the other team scored a goal. ☐

**Natalia:** I feel sad for all the fans. ☐

**Tom:** So do I. But I don't want to talk about it anymore. ☐

8 Unit

**3 Write a dialogue for each photo.**

> **Guess What!**
> It's common in spoken English to show agreement with the expression *Me too*, or for agreement with negative statements, *Me neither*. They mean the same as *So do I* and *Neither do I*.

0

0. I'm hungry.

Me too!

1

1. ______________________

______________________

2

2. ______________________

______________________

## Review

**1 Look and write a paragraph about their habits.**

1

0

2

3

4
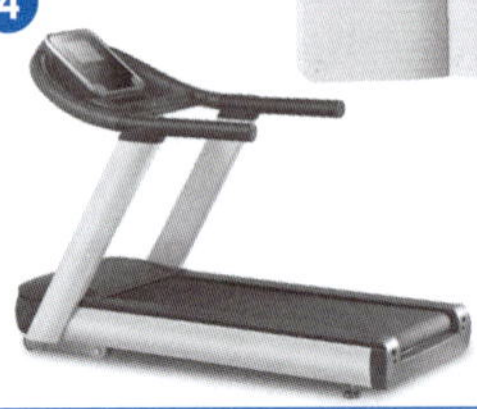

0

1

2

Are Jo and Elsie similar or different?

0. Jo orders take-out. Elsie goes out to eat.

______________________________________________

______________________________________________

______________________________________________

## Reading

**1 Read and classify the adjectives.**

casual energetic hardworking honest
lonely old retired stressed talented

# Unlikely Friendships

It's often the case that people choose friends who are like them in age, character and style. But in movies, there are often unlikely relationships between people who are appear to have nothing in common. In the 2015 comedy *The Intern,* Ben Whittaker (played by Robert De Niro) is a 70-year-old **widower** who is lonely at home and bored with **retirement**. He decides to apply for a job in a successful e-commerce clothing company owned by energetic and talented—but stressed—**entrepreneur** Jules Ostin (played by Ann Hathaway). Ben, whose previous job experience was selling telephone directories, gets the position. He shows up to work wearing a suit and a tie. Everyone else there wears casual clothes. At first, everyone at the company ignores him, but they soon learn that he's honest and hardworking, and has some valuable ideas to contribute.

The movie works well because two very different people find out that they can learn from each other—and that they do have things in common. In the end, it doesn't **matter** that they are from different generations with different views about life. It's possible to respect, like and learn from people who are different.

____
____
____
____

____
____
____
____

**2 Read, match and complete.**

0. Why does Ben apply for the job?
1. What does Jules Ostin do?
2. How old is Ben?
3. What does the company sell?
4. What do the main characters learn?

a. She's the owner of an ____ company.
b. He's ____ years old.
c. They have things in ____.
d. He is retired and lonely.
e. They sell ____ online.

**Glossary**

**widower:** a man whose wife has died

**retirement:** a stage in later life when a person doesn't work

**entrepreneur:** a person who starts his/her own business

**matter:** to be important

# Just for Fun Answer Key

## Unit 1

**1** Halloween, Independence Day, Valentine's Day, Thanksgiving

**2** *Down*: 1. Catrina 2. candles 3. turkey 4. present; *Across*: 5. diploma 6. cap 7. resolutions 8. celebrations

## Unit 2

**1** 1. F – It takes two hours! 2. T 3. T 4. F – You burn about one calorie per kilogram of body weight per hour of sleep. 5. T 6. F – It takes less than 12 hours. 7. F – It's 25%. 8. T

**2** Row 1: 1, 6, 8, 4

Row 2: 5, 2, 7, 3

## Unit 3

**1** If you turn off the water when you wash your hair, you will save up to 500 liters per month!

Buy a cloth bag and use it when you shop. If you stop using plastic bags, you will keep them out of landfills—and prevent them from polluting the environment.

If you eat chicken instead of beef, you can reduce your carbon footprint by 500%!

You don't need to buy solar panels to use clean energy. If you use natural sunlight instead of a lamp, you won't need any electricity or use any fossil fuels!

Planting trees helps the environment, but all plants do! If you keep a small plant in your house, it will produce oxygen and clean the air.

**2** Row 1: 1, 3, 2, 3

Row 2: 1, 2, 3, 2

## Unit 4

Kylie collects action figures; Olivia is a fan of a team; Will collects athletes' autographs; Jake collects movie posters; Max dresses up as video game characters

## Unit 5

**1** earthquake p. 73; lifeguards p. 72; neurons p. 74; reef p. 77; toy car p. 71

**2** his grandpa; coffee; their uncle; network; Uluru

**3** The lifeguard had hiccups. The waiter broke the glass to frighten him and cure the hiccups.

## Unit 6

**1**

N D F O T V T J Y T Q X D Z G Y
F A U K H Q H U N H Y H L F X R
S H L B I I E W E T P J O B H G
T L L G R L R J X B R Z C T H N
A O F R S X E D D R E J B V F U
R S F U T E Y E E Q A G B R Q H
T T Z B Y R R K I C D T I R E D
E Y S K G O I R A O Y Q W I W C
D Q O N B X Y U P L Q A N G R Y

**2** 1. angry 2. bored 3. cold 4. full 5. tired 6. wet

## Unit 7

**1** 1. rock climbing 2. mountain biking 3. kite surfing 4. snowboarding 5. skydiving 6. white water rafting

**2** Column 1: terrifying, thrilling, tiring

Column 3: excited, terrified, bored, interested

## Unit 8

**1** Answers will vary.

# Grammar Reference

## Present Continuous (future meaning)

We usually use the present continuous to talk about actions that are happening now. However, we can also use it to talk about future plans. We form the present continuous with the verb *be* in the present simple, and the base form of the verb with *-ing*.

- *I **am marching** in the parade tomorrow.*
- *The city **is setting off** fireworks tonight.*
- *We **are celebrating** her birthday on Saturday.*

We usually use contractions with the present continuous.

- ***I'm marching** in the parade tomorrow.*
- *The city**'s setting off** fireworks tonight.*
- *We**'re celebrating** her birthday on Saturday.*

Remember that some verbs require spelling changes. We double the consonant in verbs with a short vowel sound that end in a consonant.

- *He's **getting** his diploma this afternoon. (get)*

We remove the *–e* and add *–ing* to verbs with a long vowel that end in *–e*.

- *We're **making** resolutions at midnight. (make)*

We form the negative by adding *not* after the verb *be*.

- *She is **not** baking a pie for Thanksgiving.*
- *They are **not** opening their presents before Christmas.*

Most people use the contracted form.

- *She **isn't** baking a pie for Thanksgiving.*
- *They **aren't** opening their presents before Christmas.*

To form *Yes/No* questions, we put the verb *be* before the subject. We don't use the main verb in short answers.

- ***Is** he coming to visit later?*
- *Yes, he **is**. / No, he **isn't**.*

For *Wh-* questions, we add a question word at the beginning.

- ***When** are they arriving?*
- *After lunch.*

### *Should*

We use the modal *should* to give advice and recommendations. We use the base form of the main verb after a modal.

- *You **should eat** a lot of vegetables.*

We form the negative by adding *not* after the modal *should*. It is more common to use the contracted form.

- *We **should not** drink a lot of soda.*
- *We **shouldn't** drink a lot of soda.*

### Zero Conditional

We use the zero conditional to express facts. There are two parts of a zero conditional sentence: the condition and the consequence. The condition begins with the word *if* or *when*. When the condition comes before the consequence, there is a comma after the condition.

- ***If** you eat well**,** you feel better.*
- ***When** you eat well**,** you feel better.*

The order of the condition and the consequence can be reversed. When the condition comes after the consequence, there is no comma.

- *You feel better **if** you eat well.*
- *You feel better **when** you eat well.*

Both the condition and the consequence use the present simple tense.

- *You **sleep** better when you **don't use** a tablet before bed.*

### First Conditional

We use the first conditional to talk about future possibilities. The condition begins with the word *if* and the verb in the condition is in the present simple. We use *will* and the base form of the verb in the consequence.

- *If we* ***use*** *clean energy, there* ***will be*** *less pollution.*

As with all conditionals, the order of the condition and the consequence can be reversed.

- *There* ***will be*** *less pollution if we* ***use*** *clean energy.*

We form negative conditions by adding *don't* before the main verb.

- *If we* ***don't*** *recycle, there will be too much garbage.*

We form negative consequences by adding *won't* before the main verb.

- *If we pollute the environment, future generations* ***won't*** *have clean air or water.*

We can also form questions with conditionals.

- *If I use modern lightbulbs,* ***will I save electricity?***
- ***What will happen*** *if I listen to loud music?*

# 4 Unit

## Intensifiers

We use intensifiers to express the intensity of an adjective.

- *It was **extremely** difficult to plan the party.*
- *His costume is **so** cool.*
- *Your collection is **really** interesting.*
- *His last album was **pretty** good.*
- *I'm running **a bit** late.*

Intensifiers express a range of intensity.

extremely → !!!!
so → !!!
really → !!!
pretty → !!
a bit → !

## *Already, Yet*

We use the adverbs *already* and *yet* to talk about our expectations regarding the time of an activity. In general, we use *already* in affirmative sentences. We use *yet* in negative sentences and questions. We can use *already* and *yet* with any tense. In American English, it is common to use it with the past simple.

- *The store was **already** closed.*
- *We didn't register for the conference **yet**.*
- *Did they have lunch **yet**?*

We use *already* in a different part of the sentence than *yet*. *Already* comes after *be* or before a main verb, similar to the word *not*.

- *They are **already** late.*
- *We **already** saw that movie.*

We use *yet* at the end of a sentence or question.

- *We didn't finish our project **yet**.*
- *Did you do your homework **yet**?*

We can sometimes use *already* in questions, to express that we expect an affirmative answer.

- *Did he **already** do his homework?*

### Past Continuous

We usually use the past continuous to talk about actions that were happening over a period of time in the past. We use the past form of the verb *be* and the base form of the verb with *-ing*.

- *I **was studying** at the library.*
- *They **were playing** soccer at the park.*

Remember that some verbs require spelling changes. We double the consonant in verbs with a short vowel sound that end in a consonant.

- *He was **swimming** near the shore. (swim)*

We remove the *–e* and add *–ing* to verbs with a long vowel that end in *–e*.

- *She was **taking** photos of the sunset. (take)*

We form the negative by adding *not* after the verb *be*.

- *She was **not** waiting at the school.*
- *They were **not** eating dinner.*

Most people use the contracted form.

- *She **wasn't** waiting at the school.*
- *They **weren't** eating dinner.*

### Past Continuous: *While*

We use *while* and two past continuous clauses together to express that two ongoing activities occurred simultaneously.

- *She **was sending texts while** she **was studying**.*

### Past Continuous and Past Simple: *When*

We use the past continuous together with the past simple to express that an ongoing activity was interrupted by another activity.

- *The family **was swimming** when strong currents **pulled** them away from the beach.*

The word *when* goes before the past simple clause of the sentence.

- *The family was swimming **when strong currents pulled them away from the beach.***

### Present Perfect

We use the present perfect to talk about achievements and experiences. We use the present simple form of *have* and the past participle of the main verb.

- *She **has been** to Hawaii twice.*
- *They **have climbed** a volcano.*

Past participles can be regular or irregular. Past participles are included on the *Verb List* on page 168.

We form the negative by adding *not* after the verb *have*. Contractions are more common.

- *I **haven't** been to Hawaii before.*
- *He **hasn't** won any awards.*

### Ever

We usually use *ever* to ask about achievements and experiences.

- *Have you **ever** been to England?*

We can use short answers with the present perfect.

- *Have you ever been to England?*
- *Yes, I have.*
- *No, I haven't.*

### Already, Yet

We can use also use *already* and *yet* with the present perfect.

- *They have **already** made some friends.*
- *Has she done anything interesting **yet**?*

### *Might*

We use the modal *might* before verbs to indicate possibility.

- *I **might** take a survival course.*

The negative form also indicates possibility, or doubt that something will happen.

- *I **might not** sign up this year.*

As with other modals, we always use the base form of the main verb with *might*.

### *Would*

We use *would* for hypothetical situations in the future. It is common in questions. We can answer with short answers.

- ***Would** you eat a bug?*
- *Yes, I **would**.*
- *No, I **wouldn't**.*

### Present Perfect: *Never*

We use *never* in combination with the present perfect to emphasize that an experience has not happened at any time in the past. This is a variation of the negative form. As with *not*, *never* goes after *have* and before the past participle.

- *I've **never** eaten a bug.*
- *He's **never** learned to swim.*

### Too, Either

We can express similar opinions or circumstances using *too* and *either*. We use *too* at the end of affirmative sentences.

- *I like sushi.*
- *I like sushi* ***too****.*

We use *either* at the end of negative sentences to express similar opinions or circumstances.

- *He doesn't watch TV.*
- *I don't watch TV* ***either****.*

### So, Neither

We can also use expressions with *So* and *Neither* to express similar opinions or circumstances. With most verbs, we use the auxiliary *do* in the expression. We use *So* with affirmative sentences.

- *I* ***have*** *a headache.*
- *So* ***do*** *I.*

We use *Neither* with negative sentences. With negative sentences, the word *Neither* eliminates the need for *not*.

- *I* ***don't*** *have a calculator.*
- *Neither* ***do*** *I.*

We use *be* to express agreement with sentences with *be* as a main verb or an auxiliary verb.

- ***I'm*** *a big fan of Formula 1 racing.*
- *So* ***am*** *I.*
- *We****'re*** *studying for the math exam.*
- *So* ***are*** *we.*
- *They* ***aren't*** *going to the movies.*
- ***Neither*** *are we.*

Modals like *can, should* and *would* are also used in these expressions.

- *I* ***can*** *run a kilometer in six minutes.*
- *So* ***can*** *I.*
- *You* ***should*** *drink more water.*
- *So* ***should*** *you.*
- *I* ***wouldn't*** *eat a bug.*
- *Neither* ***would*** *I.*

### Me too, Me neither

It's common in spoken English to express similar opinions or circumstances with the expression *Me too*, or for negative sentences, *Me neither*.

- *I like dancing.*
- ***Me too.***
- *He doesn't watch TV.*
- ***Me neither.***

# Verb List

| Base Form | Past Simple | Past Participle |
|---|---|---|
| become | **became** * | **become** |
| begin | **began** | **begun** |
| believe | believed | believed |
| blow out | **blew out** | **blown out** |
| book | booked | booked |
| break | **broke** | **broken** |
| build | **built** | **built** |
| burn | **burned** | **burnt** |
| buy | **bought** | **bought** |
| catch | **caught** | **caught** |
| cause | caused | caused |
| celebrate | celebrated | celebrated |
| change | changed | changed |
| check | checked | checked |
| collect | collected | collected |
| come | **came** | **come** |
| complete | completed | completed |
| conserve | conserved | conserved |
| cry | cried | cried |
| dance | danced | danced |
| decorate | decorated | decorated |
| draw | **drew** | **drawn** |
| dress | dressed | dressed |
| drink | **drank** | **drunk** |
| drop | dropped | dropped |
| eat | **ate** | **eaten** |
| escape | escaped | escaped |
| exchange | exchanged | exchanged |
| exercise | exercised | exercised |
| explore | explored | explored |
| fall | **fell** | **fallen** |
| feed | **fed** | **fed** |
| feel | **felt** | **felt** |
| find | **found** | **found** |
| get | **got** | **gotten** |
| give | **gave** | **given** |
| go | **went** | **gone** |
| hang out | **hung out** | **hung out** |
| happen | happened | happened |
| have | **had** | **had** |
| hear | **heard** | **heard** |
| hire | hired | hired |
| improve | improved | improved |

| Base Form | Past Simple | Past Participle |
|---|---|---|
| include | included | included |
| invent | invented | invented |
| keep | **kept** | **kept** |
| laugh | laughed | laughed |
| learn | learned | learned |
| leave | **left** | **left** |
| make | **made** | **made** |
| open | opened | opened |
| order | ordered | ordered |
| pack | packed | packed |
| paint | painted | painted |
| plant | planted | planted |
| pollute | polluted | polluted |
| practice | practiced | practiced |
| prevent | prevented | prevented |
| produce | produced | produced |
| protect | protected | protected |
| provide | provided | provided |
| put | **put** | **put** |
| reach | reached | reached |
| receive | received | received |
| recycle | recycled | recycled |
| reduce | reduced | reduced |
| relax | relaxed | relaxed |
| remember | remembered | remembered |
| reuse | reused | reused |
| save | saved | saved |
| say | **said** | **said** |
| see | **saw** | **seen** |
| send | sent | sent |
| sleep in | **slept in** | **slept in** |
| start | started | started |
| stay up | stayed up | stayed up |
| stream | streamed | streamed |
| take | **took** | **taken** |
| teach | **taught** | **taught** |
| throw | **threw** | **thrown** |
| try | tried | tried |
| turn | turned | turned |
| wave | waved | waved |
| wear | **wore** | **worn** |
| work out | worked out | worked out |
| write | **wrote** | **written** |

* Irregular verbs